The Study of Dance

THE STUDY OF DANCE

JANET ADSHEAD

DANCE BOOKS LTD
9 Cecil Court London WC2

First published 1981 by Dance Books Ltd.,
9 Cecil Court, London WC2N 4EZ

© 1981 Janet Adshead

ISBN 0 903102 66 8

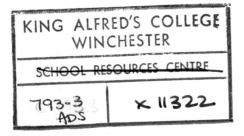
Design and production by Book Production Consultants
7 Brooklands Avenue, Cambridge CB2 2BB

Typeset by Manuset Ltd., Tranters Yard,
31 Whitehorse Street, Baldock, Herts. SG7 6QF.

Printed by The Burlington Press, Foxton, Cambridge CB2 6SW

Acknowledgements

I am very grateful to staff of a number of higher education institutions who gave willingly of their expertise at a very difficult time. A complete list appears in Appendix A. Officials of the C.N.A.A. and of the University of Leeds made information about validation procedures available with great courtesy.

In addition, a studentship from the S.S.R.C. made it financially possible to pursue a research interest on a full time basis for three years and this is acknowledged with gratitude.

I am indebted to Judith Chapman and Joan White for their meticulous reading of an earlier draft and for carefully considered and sensitively expressed comments.

My greatest debt is to June Layson (University of Leeds) for her unfailing support and encouragement over a number of years and through many versions of a Ph.D. thesis and then this text. Her comments are always a challenge to further clarity of thought and expression.

I acknowledge with gratitude the impetus towards research which David Adshead gave me, and also my parents, William and Helen Lansdale, for their support throughout the years.

Table of Contents

List of Tables

List of Diagrams

Introduction

It is hoped that teachers of dance at all levels will find something of interest here, particularly those with responsibilities for planning courses, i.e. for curriculum development in dance, whether this is ultimately for an award, of C.S.E. or an Honours degree, or within the curriculum as a non-examinable subject. Clearly there are many pitfalls which result from such a wide brief, but an attempt is made to articulate general principles which might guide curriculum choices. If some statements seem simplistic to those readers with a considerable knowledge of dance it should be borne in mind that it is necessary to set the later part of the book within a contextual and historical framework.

Dance is not taught in the abstract but within the clear constraints of a particular sector of education, whether public or private, and to people of different age groups and abilities. Some of the material presented is derived from a study of dance at a particular level of education, i.e. the higher education level and there are reasons for using this as an example. The argument here is that:

1. notwithstanding these particularities a subject called 'dance' exists and it is possible to articulate its concepts, subject matter, body of knowledge etc., independently of its application in any one instance of the educational process,
2. it is at the higher education level that one would expect to find the most clearly worked out account of what is involved in the study of any subject since, traditionally, scholarship at the highest level takes place here, not in the primary

school. Thus it is the most useful sector to examine. But having made that point there is, of course, a very close relationship between all sectors of the educational system in terms of the subject—it is *dance* which is being taught, and *wherever* it is taught one would expect to find the content that makes dance distinct from any other subject. Thus concepts and frameworks produced here have implications for any teaching of dance since they are concerned simply with dance. In addition higher education has changed so much that it might be helpful to make the information available to teachers who have to advise pupils about college applications.

It is also worth pointing out that the prejudice which the following quotation reveals about writers on dance is both prevalent and recurrent. It is also unjustifiable. The function of a dancer is to dance, of a writer to write, whether he be critic or theorist. Special skills are required in order to communicate effectively through words and these skills are not the same as those of the dancer.

Despite the youthful arrogance of Blasis, his reasons for writing a treatise on dance at the age of seventeen are interesting.* He maintains that:

> *The absence of any really valuable literature upon the subject of dancing has led me to publish this treatise. Most of the existing works are by writers who, though able men of letters, have no practical experience of dancing. These are the people to whom Berchoux refers jocundly as*
> > *. . . known for their learning, not dancers,*
> > *but most voluble about dancing.*
> *The efforts of these gentlemen, who have expended so much*

---

* There is some doubt about Blasis' date of birth but 1803 appears to be authentic. He died in 1878. His first book *An elementary treatise upon the theory and practice of the art of dancing* was first published in 1820, republished 1968 New York: Dover, translated with biographical sketch and foreword by Mary Stewart Evans.

*midnight oil upon an art of which they know nothing, are quite
useless to us.*

(Blasis, 1820, p. 4)

He claims, in company with many, that the personal
experience of dancing and making dances is of paramount
importance as a basis of producing 'valuable literature'. To
take this seriously one would have to establish that he was
concerned with increasing *understanding* of dance through
writing as well as giving a practical guide and it is taken for
granted here that it is a reasonable assumption to make. It is
evident in Blasis' own writings that he aims humbly to
expound a theory of technique, but within the next paragraph
he has expanded his ambitions to being the first to document
the 'dancer,'s art' (p. 4).

Blasis equates *knowing* the art of dance with *being able* to
dance, and there are many who would still hold this view. In
total disagreement would be the view of recent philosophers
who maintain that experience of dancing need not be a pre-
requisite for understanding and that the critical spectator may
have as valid an understanding as the performer. There are, of
course, complications with epistemology, the philosophical
area concerned with what it is to 'know' something, but the
point of quoting Blasis is to demonstrate problems which are
perennial in dance. There are seemingly irreconcilable views
which it is in part the concern of this text to examine.

It is seen to be 'a good thing' by many that practical
exponents of dance also write about it. They may or may not,
of course, have a facility with words and an appropriate
conceptual grasp of the subject since these abilities are of a
different kind from those required to perform at a high level. In
terms, for example, of the teaching of technique, Blasis may be
quite right that the distillation of years of experience may
provide a very useful teaching handbook, but in relation to
constructing valid theory, quite wrong since what dancers tend
to do is to see dance from only one, narrow point of view. In a

very important sense dancers validate theory—whether or not what they do accords with whatever principles are laid down *justifies* the theory, it is its verification in an empirical sense.

In a simpler way, unless dancers danced there would be no 'dance' and consequently nothing to study. Thus in order for study to be meaningful it must have its referents in the activity itself. Its structure, content etc., are only valid if they relate to actual dances and dancers.

But, as changing dance theories demonstrate, there is no *one* way which is valid for studying/teaching/learning dance since its manifestations are ever-evolving. What Blasis himself has to say about dance looks very odd in the light of developments since. The person who develops theoretical structures which underly the process of studying dance has an aim which is broader than 'how to do a plié'.

A frequently expressed objection to writing about dance is that it does not equate with the experience of dancing. Why it should be expected to is a mystery since they are clearly such different activities. The relationship between dancing and articulating verbally about it is complex and often metaphorical (hence the poetic element of dance criticism) but constructing valid theory is a straightforward academic exercise. Blasis obviously felt there might be a value in this and it is my concern also to demonstrate its possibilities.

It is taken as axiomatic that theoretical structures which reflect the nature(s) of dance and its varied forms are an essential base for the study of dance and for making curriculum decisions.

The book proceeds by examining arguments about the purpose and value of theoretical structures in relation to the nature(s) of the dance and the requirements of a disciplined activity in an educational system. The historical perspective in Chapter II allows consideration of the ways in which the study of dance has, as a matter of fact, developed, with particular emphasis on twentieth century Great Britain. In Chapter III major areas of change and development in the study of dance which occurred during the reorganisation of higher education in the 1970s are identified. Factual information is included as the foundation upon which to base discussion and in order that distinctions can be made, for example, between external pressures and significant trends in the subject area itself. Clearly there is interaction between these two factors. The limitations of the existing circumstances are pointed out.

In consequence a case is put forward in Chapter IV which attempts a coherent account of the totality of dance study through the notion of dance as a discipline. In Chapter V examples of the ways in which curriculum proposals might be made are derived from the dance placed in context and within historical and geographical perspectives, and some of the educational implications of so doing are discussed in Chapter VI.

1. Dance in context

Two preliminary questions which the title of the book begs are whether or not there is anything of substance to study in the area of dance and whether there is any value in doing so. In some respects it might be said unequivocally that there is something to study called 'dance' since people patently do pursue courses of study with various titles including the word dance. Nonetheless there remains a general public incredulity when one responds to the question of one's occupation by saying that one teaches dance, or one is following a masters degree in dance or doing research in dance. On the other hand it is not seen as odd to do 'dance', i.e. to dance, so why should the study of it seem strange? There are social and historical reasons why this sceptical view should be held, related to, for example, the trivialisation of dance into music hall entertainment and the prevalent social forms of dance which, like all forms of popular dance, require little formal teaching and change rapidly. More seriously the fact that dance is transient and that it has, until recently, been so rarely notated and recorded has resulted in a lack of artefacts (examples of its forms) which could be studied and in a lack of general public familiarity with many of its forms.

However, the increasing popularity of live and televised dance performances seems to indicate something of an explosion of interest on the part of the general non-dance educated public. Since anyone using this text is likely to be involved in some way with dance it is unnecessary to pursue this line further except to note that these attitudes may have prejudiced acceptance of dance as a worthwhile area of study or channelled the development of studies in dance along particular lines.

If we can accept that dance in many and varied forms exists in twentieth century societies, and that it has existed since pre-historic times, the question still has to be asked—is there any point in studying dance, is it worthwhile? Just because something exists it is not automatically of value to study it, as philosophers of education point out. Arguments for the value of studying dance must rest ultimately on the place it occupies in society, on its perceived functions and significance. Although this kind of value might seem rather remote, unless one can point to its worth in extending man's conscious horizons, in broadening understanding of life and human interaction in a global and historic sense then there is little reason to see why studies in dance might justifiably develop. Actually there is little difficulty here despite problems in the education system in recent years which have arisen from a focus on one form of dance. If one takes a historical view of dance across a number of cultures its functions are many and its perceived power enormous. Perhaps the most impressive fact is the most obvious one that as far as can be reliably ascertained man has always danced and his dance has always been important to him. The recent development of scholarly anthropological studies in dance reinforces this view.

An illustration of the range of functions that dance has been held to fulfil follows later in this chapter. Whether dance has or does *in fact* achieve these ends would be a matter for empirical evaluation. What is significant is that man has consistently *believed in* the efficacy of dance.

In many dance texts there is what seems to be an obligatory chapter on the nature and origins of dance, containing definitions, descriptions and theories as to why man dances. Attempts to locate these things are on many levels and use a variety of standpoints but the purpose is usually to persuade the reader of the importance of dance or to provide a theoretical construct for ensuing chapters. Almost inevitably the definitions that result are either so broad as to contribute nothing to one's understanding since they embrace many kinds of activity not usually thought of as dance, or so narrow that a large number of dance forms must be excluded.

However, it is a popular view that in order to study something one must be able to define it—how else can one be said to know what it means? The problem of defining dance satisfactorily might be seen more as a reflection of basic philosophical confusions than due to an elusiveness in the activity. While attempting *clarification* of the term 'dance' is valuable for intelligent understanding the assumption that there exists an *underlying essence* or single feature which is distinctive and definitive might well be misleading. Best (1974 and 1978) is helpful in pointing to the folly of attempting tight definitions. He argues cogently that to have a clear understanding of the meaning of a term does not imply being able to define it in strict terms of logical equivalence. As Best says there is confusion between 'meaning' and 'definition' here. In posing the question 'what is dance' Ellfeldt (1976) is more realistic than most writers on dance and points out that definitions usually relate to a specific form of dance and are only applicable to that form. By taking examples from dance as a magical occurrence in pre-historic times through to the present day multiplicity of art-dance forms, she exposes the particular problems for dance of attempting to present a global once and for all definition.

Since the arguments put forward in this book relate initially to any and all forms of dance no attempt is made to define. It is sufficient to say that whatever is labelled 'dance', and accepted as such by those who do it and watch it, is regarded as 'dance'. Thus questions concerning the structure, meaning or significance of particular dances, or which ask about the dance culture of different societies might offer a more secure starting point. While some fundamental features may link one form of dance with another, the form which dance takes, and its function in a given society, varies with the *context* in which it occurs.

Perhaps the oldest of these contexts is that of *ritual and religion* where dance is associated with rites of birth, initiation into adulthood, marriage and death as well as with ceremonies in praise of gods, and in propitiation of forces beyond man's conscious control, for example, the weather, alien spirits etc.

At one time, ritualistic events (and later, the Church festivals) formed the focus also of social and educational activities in the broad sense of expressing and passing on the culture of a given society. With an increasing divide between the Church and the State, representing sacred and secular forces, social forms of dance became more clearly differentiated from religious ones in Western societies. Nonetheless, some of the purposes of dance within the religious context have continued to exist in western societies under a secular heading, particularly those concerned with catharsis, with healing and with therapy. Meanwhile the 1970s have seen a revival of interest in dance as an act of worship, evidenced by the increasing number of performances in churches by both amateur and professional groups. In these instances, the amateur performances tend to be created explicitly for religious purposes, i.e. religious acts, acts of worship, while professional performances tend to be of 'works of art' based on religious themes and (sometimes) placed in a religious building—in other words the religious nature of the performance is secondary to the artistic purpose.

The *social* context of dance forms the second major strand and includes the ever changing popular forms of dance which are manifest in all societies. Their purpose is one of increasing social cohesion, reinforcing group values, giving expression to festival and celebration and providing a socially acceptable marriage market. There is nothing new in any of these functions; Arbeau, writing in 1588, stated that:

> . . . *dancing is practised to reveal whether lovers*
> *are in good health and sound of limb*
>
> *(p.12)*

and there is evidence to show that dance has performed these functions since pre-Christian times. It is, perhaps, this form of dance, which is easily accessible to most people that seems least academically respectable as an area of study to the average person since one needs a pair of historical/sociological spectacles to perceive its continuing importance for man.

5

The third context is one in which, like the social context, dance had an independent existence before Christianity, that is, in the Greek theatre. A *theatre* form of dance re-emerged as a development from social dance forms in Western Europe during the time of Louis XIV (1638-1715). Dance as court ritual was of significance both socially and artistically. The two were intertwined in that social graces were, to some extent, elevated to an art form, embellished with gesture and embodied in elaborate court dances.

However, the performance of dance on a stage by specially trained dancers grew into the highly technical, structured form of classical ballet and adopted the characteristics of a theatrical form. The context of theatre lends a particular emphasis and focus to works presented and ballet developed in a similar way to other theatre art forms, for example, drama. The twentieth century has seen the growth of many diverse forms of theatre dance, the most widespread of these being located under the umbrella term of modern dance.

2. Dance as a subject of study

Related to both artistic and social contexts is the development of dance in education. While it is a major consideration it is of a different order from the three contexts so far discussed. Before the development of educational institutions for the whole population (in Western European countries) the purposes of education were concomitant with those of socialisation. While some would argue that education *is* socialisation and few would deny any link, the education system in the twentieth century embodies more specific aims in the development and education of the next generation than purely those of socialisation.

A major area of society in which dance may be found is, then, within the educational system of schools, colleges and universities. It is in this sphere that the interest of the present writer lies. Within the educational system one would expect to find the most coherent account of the totality of dance study, i.e. a theoretical basis from which any manifestation of dance might be approached and studied, taking account of the context in which it operates.

In attempting to locate a 'coherent' account of an area of human interest one is, of course, doing something which is one stage removed from the actual activity. The reasons for doing this perhaps need some justification since many practitioners of dance regard theorising as remote and peripheral. It is argued here that a coherent theoretical structure is necessary for *any* subject which is put forward for inclusion in an overcrowded curriculum or for the award of a qualification, be it C.S.E.* or an Honours degree.

A particular view of education is implicit in these statements, i.e. that it is a rational, articulate process which is necessarily open to public validation. However, the division of experience and understanding into specific realms called 'subjects' or 'disciplines' or 'forms of knowledge' which might be said to be discrete units reflecting some internal logic is more problematic and open to debate. Since it is the aim of the book to arrive at an account of the totality of dance studies it is necessary to pursue this point further in order to provide a framework against which the emergence of dance as a 'discipline' or subject in its own right might be seen. Theories of knowledge are, of course, the province of philosophers and there is no pretence of philosophical expertise here, merely a bringing together of ideas which may inform a theory of dance studies.

What then might be the salient features of a discipline? One immediate distinction made by some writers is between a process, i.e. a disciplined activity, a way of doing something in a rigorous manner, and a body of facts to be learned, derived from pre-existing knowledge in some absolute sense. Traditionally, greater emphasis has been placed in the educational system on theoretical areas of human enquiry and on facts to be learned than on practical or artistic activities and

*Certificate of Secondary Education

7

processes. There are several possibilities here; one might attach the label 'discipline' to a logically distinct form of knowledge (if such exist—see references at the end of the chapter to Hirst and Best, etc.), or to an established curriculum area (which may not be the same thing), in a university or in a school (which may again be different).

Much energy has been expended by philosophers of education in attempting to delineate discrete areas of knowledge. Confusion for people involved in practical activities has arisen because of, for example, Hirst's insistence on the logical priority of propositional knowledge. Nonetheless, Hirst includes in his characterisation of a discipline non-propositional elements such as skills, attitudes etc. (1974, p.97).

A parallel problem for newly developed subject areas has been the philosophical insistence on uniqueness (less emphasised now) which insists on trying to establish what is 'unique' about an area of study. In the case of dance, which developed in the education system under the aegis of Physical Education, the major related areas have been those of Human Movement Studies (H.M.S.) or Physical Education (P.E.). Dance itself fares much better than H.M.S. or P.E. under this pressure for clarification but it is even so a dubious exercise to search for 'essences' or single features which characterise activities.

At the other end of a spectrum of ideas about disciplines Pring (1976) argues that they are simply well organised areas of study and that a Hirstian approach fails to take account of the complex differences between disciplined enquiries into different kinds of problems.

Pring offers four features of a disciplined activity: these are that

(i)   there are central organising concepts

(ii)   there are principles of procedure which are appropriate to the activity in question

(iii)   there are criteria of success which arise from notions of excellence in a sphere

(iv)   there is a group of problems and interests which
         provide the disciplining framework of enquiry.
Further references to this area of debate may be found at the
end of this chapter but it is pertinent here to relate the
discussion to issues in dance.

It will become evident in later chapters that the character of
dance as taught in educational institutions has, between 1950
and 1980, undergone considerable change. One of the changes
has been towards a greater emphasis upon dance as an art
form, i.e. in a theatrical and artistic context so it is worthwhile
examining the implications of this shift. While there are other
problems which arise from the move away from P.E. and
H.M.S. it at least allows for a focus on the particular problems·
and character of creating and performing art, of experiencing,
appreciating and evaluating a work of art—in this case a
dance. But there are then further problems which adhere to the
difficult area of art/aesthetic education, notably the emphasis
of many artists and theoreticians on personal (subjective)
response which, although beyond the scope of this book, raises
questions about the validity of education in the arts. (For an
interesting debate on the issue see Best and Reid, *British
Journal of Aesthetics,* Vol. 20, No. 2, Spring, 1980). If dance
places itself firmly in the arts realm then it also takes on a
collection of philosophical problems which are the basis of
aesthetics, broadly concerning the concepts of art and the
aesthetic, the function of art, and the existence and nature of
aesthetic judgements etc.

The transient nature of some of the arts, i.e. music, drama,
opera and dance, adds a further dimension, that of
interpretation through performance, since it is a crucial
characteristic of dance that it requires performance in order to
exist in time.

3. Dance and problems of knowledge

The purpose of introducing these preliminary points about

dance is in order to demonstrate that there are particular knowledge problems which one has to face in order to put forward a coherent structure for dance as an art. Clearly this is a development of the earlier discussion of what kind of thing a discipline might be. (For more detailed accounts see references at the end of the chapter.) Since the acquisition of knowledge (whether 'coming to know', 'knowing', 'knowledge about', 'knowing how to' etc.) in the development of 'mind' and 'persons' is fundamental to educational aims and appears as a requirement in all accounts of subjects, in some form, it is important to examine briefly some of the characteristics of what is termed 'knowledge'.

The traditional view, which Hirst developed, divides knowledge into seven distinct forms. He equates knowledge with true propositions which can be classified in terms of the concepts, logical structure and the criteria for truth that they employ. The 1974 version of his theory is easily accessible and there is little point in repeating his arguments. It is pertinent to point out that Hirst concerns himself with a small area of the concept of knowledge and one which may have little relevance for the arts—at least in the sense in which people have sought to use his theories (i.e. in making statements *about* works of art). However, his notion that the work of art itself is a statement equal to a true proposition, is of interest. There is certainly a case to be made that it is possible to make true propositions (statements) *about* dance which can be evaluated as true or false in the normal academic manner by pointing to publicly available criteria. These statements might concern any aspect of dance.

Secondly, it is possible to argue that knowing *how* to dance, how to choreograph and how to interpret or appreciate a dance involves more than knowing a number of facts. In some cases it involves physical skill at a high level (to dance) or understanding of, and facility with, choreographic processes etc. etc. The point here is merely to indicate that 'knowing' in dance is not a simple matter but a complex way of using different sources of information and skills which combine to allow one to say of someone that she knows how to dance, or knows about this or that dance. There are difficult problems but the crucial thing is to restore procedural knowledge, i.e. learning how to work within the framework of the activity of dance, to its rightful place. Procedural knowledge might be used in order to talk/write/theorise about dance or to dance or evaluate/appreciate it. In other words there are specific, appropriate ways of going about it which are determined by the activity itself (again, see Pring). Of course one might work within the confines of a discipline such as history and apply it to dance, and to some extent all subjects are dependent upon the insights of other disciplines (with the possible exception of mathematics), but the search here is for the central organising concepts of dance itself, in terms of which historical (or any other kind of) study might take place.

For the purposes of this study into the nature of dance as a discipline the term 'discipline' might be characterised in the following way. It is seen to be important that there exists a coherent collection of ideas, objects and/or experiences which justify interest and close examination. Clearly the content of the discipline depends upon the particular problems which it is concerned to examine. It is argued that this examination might be theoretical (in making statements about), practical (in learning how to make, create or perform) and/or evaluative (in learning how to criticise, appraise, make judgements about). A discipline with these features contains notions of standards applicable to understanding theoretical structures and revealed in the ability to apply principles of procedure in practice, and in making judgements within the framework of the activity.

One of the presuppositions of this approach is that the number of possible 'disciplines' is not theoretically limited. The basis of this is that the ways in which man has come to organise experience are many and varied and still open to change. Education and the arts are both areas of dynamic change, responsive to pressures in society. It is then possible to

11

recognise that new areas of interest arise, for example the growth of modern dance in relation to other performing arts, which has given rise to a new area of study which coheres about the idea of 'performance'.

Within the arts the coherent collections of ideas, objects and experiences which justify interest and close examination are those respectively of aesthetics, works of art and the making and appreciating of them. The particular problems with which the arts are concerned are to be found in the various media used; the skills and techniques required for making and performing; the processes of composition through which materials are manipulated into structural wholes; standards and criteria of appraisal and evaluation both internally and within the larger social and historical context.

Thus to claim, as the literature and evidence of the 1970s does, that dance is a structured, disciplined area of study within the arts, it must be demonstrated that these processes, skills and techniques exist, in relation to composition, performance and interpretation. In addition there would have to be criteria against which performances and statements made about them might be evaluated.

If one wished to justify dance on other grounds, e.g. social benefits etc., then a further exercise is required in terms of the social sciences.

Summary

In summary one can conclude that the activity of dancing and making dances has had considerable significance for mankind throughout time. This significance has been of a ritual, social and artistic nature. If the study of dance within the educational system is justified in any or all of these terms then structures are required which lay out the relevant concepts, the methods of procedure etc. which are appropriate to study. Selection from such a map of the study possibilities in dance is then part of the curriculum process, based on priorities of individual situations.

Recommended reading

Knowledge and the arts

Best, D. (1974) *Expression in movement and the arts.* London: Lepus.

Best, D. (1978) *Philosophy and human movement.* London: Allen and Unwin.

Best, D. and Reid, L.A. (1980) Article and reply, *British Journal of Aesthetics,* Vol. 20, No. 2, Spring, pp. 115-127, 165-170.

Hirst, P.H. (1974) *Knowledge and the curriculum.* London: R.K.P.

Pring, R. (1976) *Knowledge and schooling.* London: Open Books.

Reid, L.A. (1974) The arts as a unique form of knowledge, *Cambridge Journal of Education,* Vol. 4, No. 3, pp. 153-165.

Urmson, J.O. (1976) The performing arts, in Lewis, H.D. (Ed.) *Contemporary British Philosophy* 4th series, pp. 239-252. London: Allen and Unwin.

Dance

Arbeau, T. (1588, 1967) *Orchesography.* Trans. Mary Stewart Evans, revised J. Sutton. New York: Dover.

Backman, E.L. (1952) *Religious dances in the Christian church and in popular medicine.* London: Allen and Unwin.

Cohen, S.J. (1974) *Dance as a theatre art.* New York: Dodd Mead.

Cunningham, J. (1965) *Dancing in the inns of court.* London: Jordon.

Ellfeldt, L. (1976) *Dance from magic to art.* Iowa: Brown.

Hanna, J.L. (1979) *To dance is human.* Austin: University of Texas.

Oesterley, W.O.E. (1923, 1968) *The sacred dance.* New York: Dance Horizons.

Royce, A.P. (1977) *The anthropology of dance.* London: Indiana University.

Rust, F. (1969) *Dance in society.* London: R.K.P.

The questions which immediately follow from Chapter I then are: does dance have these structures and, if so, what are they, and how have they developed? What assumptions or basic premises underlie them? In starting with a historical view one hopes to locate the earliest attempts to study dance, and this is most likely to have happened during the era in which dance became, in some highly regarded forms, something which not everyone did as a matter of course, but which was the province of a specialist group of performers.

For the sake of convenience the chapter is divided into two sections since a briefer overview is presented of the period before the twentieth century than of developments so far in this century.

1. A historical view of the study of dance up to 1900

It may be possible anthropologically to find examples of specialist roles within the dance which were taught only to certain individuals but it is difficult to find evidence of the kind of codification which might demonstrate the intention to *study* dance. Although descriptive texts on dance were written earlier (e.g. that of Arbeau, 1588) it is not until the seventeenth century that one finds substantial evidence of structured observation and analysis of dance preserved in writing. The development of printing was, of course, crucial in this. The writings of the dancing masters and dance theorists of the seventeenth and eighteenth centuries represent some of the earliest attempts to make sense of the dance. The very existence of a 'dancing master' implies that set dances and forms existed and that specific steps were taught.

Arbeau, writing in 1588, describes the dance as 'honourable exercise' and combines descriptions of dances with social homilies and comments upon 'gracefulness' in the dance— perhaps a beginning of the aesthetics of dance, but more closely tied to the social context. John Playford's 1651 publication, *The English Dancing Master* is certainly the most famous of the early attempts to describe the steps of country dances. His introduction illustrates the functions which the dance might serve and while they might seem a little odd to a twentieth century reader, they should be seen in the context of the increasing urbanisation of society and the development of a 'class' society at that time. Rituals and patterns of behaviour which might serve to differentiate one group from another were of importance particularly to those striving for a higher place in society. Thus Playford states in his introduction that the dance is:

. . . *excellent for recreation, after more serious studies, making the body active and strong, graceful in deportment and a quality very much beseeming a gentleman.*

The social significance of dance is emphasised, and it is interesting to note that its primary use is *recreative* and a *contrast* to serious study. A notion of education is evident which has therapeutic overtones as well as social aims.

While Playford is content to describe the structure of the dances as an aid to learning, de Lauze, writing earlier, in 1623, placed greater emphasis on the social appropriateness of aspects of the dance. The ritual and complexity attached to the bow exemplifies this and de Lauze describes the intricate variations required on meeting people of superior and inferior status and in greeting men or women. In an age when the manners of the court were becoming increasingly artificial, the observance of the correct mode of behaviour was of the utmost importance.

During the seventeenth century court masques reached a high level of spectacular extravagance in which the dancing of ordinary members of the court was not always good enough for Louis XIV. Thus in 1661 he established the Royal Academy of Dancing. The relationship between the ballroom dancing of the time and the court ballet (between 1615 and 1641) is well described by Christout (1964). She maintains that the bodily requirements were similar but that the forms diverged in terms of technical standards and of spectacle. The link between social and artistic contexts, is nonetheless close. Even Ebreo, a fifteenth century dancing master, writing long before Louis XIV, called social dances the *art* of dancing and contrasted the upper class forms with those of the common people who:

> . . . *with depraved minds turn it from a liberal art and virtuous science, into a vile adulterous affair.*

(Kinkeldy, 1929, p. 8)

To return to the actual texts, the descriptions of steps in the dance were most usually through a word or phrase which, presumably, was readily understood at the time. However, even the early writers were aware of the problems of giving accurate descriptions that could be unequivocally understood. Technical terms were devised which presupposed practical expertise. Arbeau supplemented words with drawings, other writers with stick figures, while Feuillet laid out the floor patterns by means of linear diagrams and movements of the body by a system of symbols relating to parts of the body.

Dancing masters were a vital part of society, developing new dances as well as teaching existing ones. Some agreement on terminology became necessary and the search began for a system of analysing and recording movement, from which a group of writers who might be called 'dance theorists' emerged. The title is given because they attempted to create a coherent theory of dance in addition to their work of making and teaching dances.

John Weaver, who lived from 1673 to 1760, related the movements of the dance and their expressive potential to the working of the human body—an approach clearly evident in the title of his 1721 publication *Anatomical and mechanical lectures upon dancing.* This particular orientation to dance theory has continued and would today be located in anatomical, physiological, kinesiological and biomechanical analyses of human movement. Despite the mechanical orientation of this text Weaver was mainly concerned with dance as an art form.

Noverre's concerns (1727-1810) were rather different. He acknowledged the importance of an understanding of anatomy but placed more emphasis on expression. His concern for 'natural expression' should be seen though in the context of the highly stylised form of dance in existence at the time. Noverre created dances which were dramatic and unified wholes based on a theme rather than a series of highly technical interludes unrelated to each other which was the normal pattern. In his text *Letters on dancing and ballets* pub. 1803 one finds a sustained attempt to develop a theory of the meaning and significance of dance in an artistic context.

While Noverre might be said to have been primarily concerned with choreography and the aesthetics of dance, Carlo Blasis (1803-1878) is noted for the structure he gave to performing skills. He produced in 1820 an early attempt to systematise a technique for ballet, in his book (already quoted on p. xii) *An elementary treatise upon the theory and practice of the art of dancing.* He makes it clear that certain theoretical principles underlie the practical performance of ballet, notably the outward turn of the legs, the five positions, related leg gestures, attitudes of the body, the position and carriage of the arms. The emphasis within his text is on the 'proper' performance of stated steps and gestures to achieve grace and elegance.

Thus Weaver, Noverre and Blasis attempted to structure the dance in its theatrical context, while earlier writers such as Arbeau and Playford laid more emphasis on its social functions. Delsarte (1811-1871) continues the tradition of dance theorists. His influence upon modern dance has been substantial despite the fact that his primary concern was with everyday movement. Delsarte's movement theories were fundamentally based on metaphysical speculation about the trinity of life, mind and soul. He was concerned to establish how meaning is externalised in movement and his theoretical structures resulted in three 'orders of movement' and nine subsidiary laws governing the significance of motion. Stebbins (1886) describes his theories in detail and refers to the various systems of gymnastics which developed from his work while Shawn's publications in 1946 and 1963 provide the link with modern American dance. Of particular interest in the light of twentieth century developments is Delsarte's theory of the relationship between movement and emotion, or between mental states and gesture. Delsarte's approach then is psychological in tenor while based on metaphysical premises. The emphasis on harmony and the therapeutic effect of following the various Delsarte-derived systems links the nineteenth century with the more recent development of 'life enhancing' movement activities. It illustrates a quite different context from those of the theatre and of social values described earlier.

Thus it is clear (brief as the account given here is—it functions merely as a reminder of the history of dance) that by the beginning of the twentieth century embryonic structures were in evidence. They developed not because anyone specifically wanted to put the teaching of dance on the school map, education for the whole population was only just beginning, but out of continuing human curiosity about the structure and logic of dances, and of human behaviour in the creation of such phenomena. The theoretical structures which did exist reflected the concerns of dance in each different context. While dance in a religious context was, by the mid nineteenth century, little in evidence in the Western world, travellers' tales of Eastern countries were beginning to arouse anthropological interest which revealed again the link between dance and religion. In the western world social and artistic contexts were more clearly separated and while dance in the social context emphasised simple steps and socially valuable interchange, dance in the artistic context stressed a high technical standard of performing skills and the expressive characteristics of a theatre art.

These examples illustrate how dance itself, manifest in a

variety of contexts, gives rise to structures which are appropriate for understanding *that* form of dance in *that* situation. It makes the development of a peculiarly 'educational' form of dance in the twentieth century both unremarkable (to be expected with the development of an education system) and at the same time very odd since it bore so little relationship to other forms of dance.

2. Dance in the educational context 1900-1970

The second part of this chapter attempts to trace developments in the study of dance within the educational system. Of necessity this is a superficial account in itself but references are given for deeper study. The main trends which are evident are, firstly, that dance studies adopted a psychological/therapeutic base in the early part of the century and eventually culminated in a form of dance known as 'modern educational dance'. Secondly, reappraisals of the validity of the arguments used to support this form of dance occurred in the 1960s and 1970s, as a result of which dance studies emerged with a strong art/ aesthetic orientation.

Between 1900 and 1945 schooling became generally available and as far as dance existed at all its main purpose was social. In the late nineteenth and early twentieth centuries the reasons given for including dance in the school timetable were chiefly concerned with social poise, grace and physical development. Grove, writing in 1895 in her book *Dancing*, re-introduced a therapeutic element in suggesting that dance might 'brighten the mind of the backward child' (p. 382), 'the sulky perforce throw off their habitual mood' (p. 383), the dance might give pleasure to the deaf and dumb and help in disciplining the naughty child. The polemics of the period make interesting reading.

The revival of interest in older folk forms instigated by Cecil Sharp at the turn of the century also emphasised the recreative, physical and social aspects of dance. These revivals were of

21

country dances in the style of Playford, which demanded study of the original writings and prompted further research into existing country dances in various parts of the British Isles and the U.S.A.

As one might expect, it is in the educational system (both private and public) at its different levels that the *study* of dance developed and theoretical structures became evident. Notions of what it is to be 'educated' clearly influence the choice of curriculum activities and the way in which they are taught, thus forms of dance which exemplify the general aims of educators are likely to thrive. However, ideas of what education should be about change, for example, whether the emphasis is upon the child or the subject. What is appropriate at primary level might be different in emphasis from secondary level and again at higher education level. Since it is at the level of higher education (post 'A' level) that one would expect to find the most comprehensive and detailed account of structures for the study of dance, it is chiefly in this area that the evidence presented here is located and examined. However, until the 1970s dance in higher education was studied mainly in the context of training teachers, which gave it a particular orientation.

Between 1900 and 1930 a number of modern dance forms came into existence in England arising from the inspiration of Isadora Duncan. Although they were ostensibly separate theatre forms, their origins had similarities in relation to the ideas of ancient Greece and their justifications in education were very similar (for further information see Layson, 1970). Eurhythmics, Euchorics, Expression Gymnastics, Natural Movement, Margaret Morris Movement and the Revived Greek Dance are examples of the proliferation of movement forms, all of which had some influence on dance education both in state schools and in the private sector where schools are devoted to dance training for performance.

In broad summary perhaps the central notion which emerged from all these forms was the importance of portraying feeling through bodily movement. In turn this influenced dance as taught in schools, reflecting a changing orientation in educational philosophy from the subject to the child particularly at primary level.

Although the notion of 'expression' does not necessarily only mean *self* expression the psychological thread described earlier (e.g. the work of Delsarte) focused attention on this aspect and continued through the work of Laban (1879-1958) who lived and worked in Germany and then in England. He developed theories of a balanced and harmonious personality related to specific movement qualities or 'effort' elements. Although these theories have had considerable impact on the teaching of dance in schools in England, Laban was not solely concerned with this aspect of movement and at various times worked in the theatre, in association with industry and with recreative and educational groups. He is perhaps best described as a hypothesiser who analysed movement and developed a system for notating it (Kinetography Laban or Labanotation). His theories encompass a wide range of approaches to the study of movement which has been both a strength and a weakness of the work as it has subsequently been developed by others.

Laban's basic text *Modern educational dance* (1948) sought to explain the underlying theory of his teaching through what were termed the 'sixteen movement themes'. These themes, later expanded, became the basis of teaching modern educational dance, developed and clarified by Preston-Dunlop (1963). Laban's analysis of movement focused around four distinct though connected aspects of movement; the action of the body, the quality with which it moves, the spatial location of its movements and relationships between parts of the body, movements and individuals.

Although the metaphysical foundations of Laban's theories are open to criticism, and are no longer regarded as a necessary basis of the work, the structure which he established for the observation and analysis of movement has proved particularly relevant in creative approaches to movement education (in

23

which he included dance) and, to a lesser extent, in industry.

However, the large range of application of Laban's theories has led to confusion over the purposes of movement in the education of the child although contributing to the growth of more discrete areas of study. For example, investigations into man's everyday movement patterns have furthered nineteenth century links with psychology and therapeutic aspects of medicine. Similarly, sociological and anthropological studies have developed which are concerned with the significance of movement in communication.

A theory of movement, however, is not sufficient for a theory of dance although it undoubtedly is a necessary part of such a theory and Laban's published writings stopped short of a fully developed dance theory.

In addition to this broad movement orientation dance was adopted in the state education system under the auspices of physical education which further emphasised the movement aspect, since all activities under the aegis of physical education share this common element. Psychological and sociological arguments in support of child-centred education were popular and led to what might be seen as a distortion of the original claim made by Jordan (1938) for dance as part of art education. The resultant emphasis was on the innate urge of children to dance spontaneously, on the child's own experience of moving and on the improvement of communication and social interaction through dance. During the period 1935 to 1970 modern educational dance became the form of dance most usually taught in schools and colleges.

However, partly as a consequence of the development of the B.Ed. degree in the 1960s, there has been an attempt to examine critically the assumptions underlying the teaching of modern educational dance. The seminal works in this area are Layson (1970) and Redfern (1973) which, through different approaches, examine the concepts, theories and validity of the claims made for modern educational dance as an educational activity. It is interesting to note that specifically *educational* reasons (i.e. concerned with the development of the personality and with social interaction) were being put forward to justify the existence of a new *form* of dance.

Claims made for the educational value of modern educational dance may be grouped under five main headings (see Layson, 1970). Each claim is stated here and then discussed briefly.

1. **That movement forms are universal**, i.e. that mankind shares a common potential for moving.

   This hardly constitutes a justification for any form of dance in education since (i) moving is not self-evidently of value, and (ii) not all movement is dance.

2. **That children have an innate urge to move**, i.e. that they spontaneously leap, run etc.

   This is justified under a particular educational philosophy which approves anything that is 'natural' and its development. Further, the assumption that movement of this kind is the same as, or is related in some significant way to modern educational dance is unargued and would need to be demonstrated in order to constitute a serious claim.

3. **That there is a beneficial effect upon the child from experiencing a wide range of movement qualities** termed 'efforts' by Laban, which is capable of contributing to the personality development of the child.

   This claim is seen to rest upon assumptions concerning the relationship between movement characteristics and personality traits which some would argue are unjustified, or at best yet to be adequately demonstrated.

4. **That modern educational dance is unique in offering many opportunities for small group interaction**, in encouraging co-operation and improving communication.

   In dismissing this claim it is argued that although dance is frequently performed within a group, the untested, implicit assumption is that the kind of interaction involved and relationships established are of the same order as those in everyday life and that there is some transfer from the one situation to the other. This point is disputed by Redfern (1973) on logical grounds. She argues that if the form of dance termed 'modern educational dance' is concerned with establishing a symbolic and virtual form of communication rather than with the representation of actual life situations, then the relationships which evolve are not for the purpose of socialisation but subservient to the demands of the emerging dance form. However, some would argue that the teaching approach most usually used, i.e. a creative, shared approach, may well have value in an educational sense.

5. **That the form of dance taught in schools** (whether termed modern educational dance, modern dance or creative dance) **is essentially an aesthetic experience** and that it has potentially the structure of an art form.

   While acknowledging that some forms of dance have functioned mainly for social purposes (e.g. folk dance) some writers on dance in education would claim that the form of dance taught most nearly resembles the theatre form of modern dance. If a wide range of dance forms is taught the most appropriate title might, therefore, be 'dance' and all forms could be justified as part of aesthetic (as distinct from art) education. That is, while all forms of dance might be said to have aesthetic potential they are not necessarily art. If a form of dance similar to that in the theatre, e.g. ballet or modern dance, is taught, then it is argued that the justification might be within the realm of art education since dance in the theatre is accepted as an art. It follows (for example in Redfern's writings) that modern dance in education must be concerned with developing the abilities of the child and the student to manipulate the material of dance, i.e. movement, in the making of structured wholes that have some meaning for both the performer and spectator, and with the appreciation of created forms, that is, with a product as well as a process.

A consequence of these considerations of the claims made has been a tendency to refer to 'modern dance' in preference to 'modern educational dance', the latter being seen as pretentious and unjustifiable.

Publications after 1970 may still be examined and evaluated under these headings and the changing emphasis is even more evident. As the nature of modern dance in education has been more tightly defined within the art/aesthetic umbrella, so the many claims for it have been reduced. It might be seen as a further consequence that modern dance is then one form of dance among many. As a result other forms may be further defined and in fact now occur more widely in education, with appropriate justifications resurrected and modified from the original claims made for modern educational dance. For example, a later article by Redfern (1975) analyses the social contribution of some forms of dance.

Modern dance, placed within the realm of art, is susceptible to further change since the end product, the dance, is of at least as much importance as the process of creating it, and questions are therefore raised concerning standards, techniques, choreographic devices, criteria for criticism and the relevance of the spectator, i.e. the areas arising from an artistic context. Dance then somehow has to satisfy both artistic and educational criteria (see Chapter I).

The advent of the B.Ed. degree in the 1960s offered an opportunity to reconsider the content of dance courses. Courses for the fourth year of study were to be of an academic nature bringing the work in education and a main subject to degree standard. The question arose of what constituted degree level work in the areas of dance and physical education (the latter sometimes subsumed dance). Whereas prior to this time courses were largely of a practical nature concerned with the acquisition of appropriate bodily skills, the understanding of

Laban's movement theories and the elucidation of suitable teaching content and method for schools, the new B.Ed. courses had to demonstrate the existence of a coherent body of knowledge which could be examined in the traditional form of three hour essay type examinations as well as in practical examinations. Conflicting views were expressed about the significance and relevance of practical work in relation to degree level studies and these arguments continue still.

These developments prompted debate about the nature(s) of dance and physical education and a quest for the fundamental concepts and structure of the subjects. In the 1960s conferences were organised which brought together theoreticians from other disciplines (e.g. philosophy, aesthetics, and sociology) and dance and P.E. lecturers in an attempt to clarify subject areas and in particular to locate relevant theoretical constructs. The search for a classification system and theoretical structure which would illuminate all man's activities in which moving is the central component was the beginning of a new interdisciplinary field of study called 'Human movement studies'.

Human movement studies has since emerged with three main strands: (i) the *academic* study of human movement which draws on the separate and distinctive modes of thought of the physical and human sciences and philosophy, (ii) the *practical* engagement in forms of movement, and (iii) the *applied* study of human movement, for example in education. Physical education then becomes a set of practical theories used in the formulation of principles for the practice of teaching while human movement studies, freed from practical functions, may develop its own standards, areas of study and procedures. Discrete areas of study have developed, for example, motor impairment, physical growth and degeneration, movement analysis and aesthetics and human movement (see Brooke and Whiting, 1973).

Illustrating the trend towards investigations of a theoretical nature into dance, the A.T.C.D.E. (1973) publications of papers read at conferences between 1970 and 1973 include sociological, anthropological and philosophical perspectives on dance.

The increasing emphasis on dance as an art form has moved dance in education further away from physical education. While both could be subsumed in different ways under human movement studies, dance could be, and is, increasingly subsumed under the arts.

Forces for change in the direction of art which are outside the educational system but which nonetheless affect it are found in the increase of Graham-derived modern dance productions in the theatre following the establishment of the London Contemporary Dance Theatre and the change of orientation of the Rambert Company. Demonstration groups from dance companies undertook visits to educational establishments in the mid 1970s giving an image of dance which bore little relation to Laban-derived dance. There has also been considerable activity in the somewhat ill-defined area between on the one hand, the professional dance company and on the other, dance as part of the school or college curriculum. Dance, like drama, has increasingly appeared in local communities performed by amateurs or small groups of semi-professionals. Locally based arts organisations have emerged which tend to encourage interaction at a more personal level between the educator, professional artist, student and child.

These factors have prompted discussion of the nature of the dance taught in the education system in relation to that which is found in the theatre and in society in general. As Redfern (1975) asks, what kind of dance is most appropriate for schools given the bewildering variety of forms in existence?

The Schools Council working party on Arts and the Adolescent (1975) confirmed that there was considerable confusion on the part of teachers concerning the aims of dance education. Conclusions were drawn that dance had been severely hindered by its dependence on physical education. In addition, confusion arises from the problem common to all performing arts in education of the balance between the child as a performer of others' work, the child as a creator of new forms and the child as spectator. This confusion is revealed in the aims of dance teachers who tend to focus either on the physical development of the child through dance or on the child's aesthetic and emotional development through the creation and appreciation of form. The report on dance concludes by saying that:

> . . . *there is a clear need for a more rigorous investigation of dance education . . . and for some definite reappraisal of the lead and direction given by colleges.*
>
> (Schools Council, 1975, p. 55)

The central question that the report asks is, what kind of teachers for what kind of curriculum? The project report stated that:

> . . . *all discussion of content, method, materials and organisation hinged upon a satisfactory account being given of the function of the arts in the education of children in school,*
>
> (p. 66)

and it attempted to establish a conceptual framework for such a curriculum, based on the belief that the arts have the power to expand man's conscious horizons; to challenge and disturb; to cause man to remake his image of the world and himself, and in this sense are valuable in education.

Summary

Having suggested in Chapter I that certain requirements have to be met in order to make a case for dance as a disciplined area of study, questions were then posed concerning existing structures for dance study. A historical account of the development of the study of dance reveals general trends towards an art orientation intermittently interrupted by social or personal development aims. Systematic attempts to describe and analyse the movements of the dance were located within the artistic, ritual·and social contexts in which the dance itself existed. With the growth of education for the total population theories of education influenced the way in which modern forms of dance were adopted and, to some extent, mitigated against a comprehensive theory for the study of dance since it did not have a parallel growth outside teacher education. By 1970 dance study was beginning to adopt an artistic/aesthetic base within a degree award in higher education. The curriculum questions are still in abeyance since dramatic changes in the 1970s caused further developments in dance study. Embryonic structures were given a further impetus towards clarification by external pressures.

Recommended reading

Pre-twentieth century

Arbeau, T. (1588, 1967) *Orchesography*. Trans. Mary Stewart Evans. Revised J. Sutton. New York: Dover.

Blasis, C. (1820) *An elementary treatise upon the theory and practice of the art of dancing*. New York: Dover, 1968.

Christout, M-F. (1964) *The court ballet in France 1615-1641*, *Dance Perspectives*, No. 20.

De Lauze, F. (1623) *Apologie de la danse*. Trans. J. Wildeblood. London: Muller, 1952.

Kinkeldy, O. (1929) *A Jewish dancing master of the Renaissance: Guglielmo Ebreo*. New York: Dance Horizons.

Noverre, J.G. (1803) *Letters on dancing and ballets*. New York: Dance Horizons, 1968.

Playford, J. (1651) *English dancing master*. New York: Dance Horizons, repub. of 1933, ed. 1975.

Shawn, T. (1963) *Every little movement*. New York: Dance Horizons.

Stebbins, G. (1886, 1977) *Delsarte system of expression*. New York: Dance Horizons.

Twentieth century

A.T.C.D.E. Dance section (1973) *Collected conference papers.*

Brooke J.D. and Whiting H.T.A. (Ed.) (1973) *Human movement—a field of study.* London: Lepus.

Jordan, D. (1938) *The dance as education.* London: O.U.P.

Laban, R. (1948, 1963, 1975) *Modern educational dance.* London: MacDonald & Evans.

Layson, J. (1970) The contribution of modern dance to education. University of Manchester: unpublished M.Ed. thesis.

Preston-Dunlop, V. (1963, 1980) *A handbook for modern educational dance.* London: MacDonald & Evans.

Redfern, H.B. (1973) *Concepts in modern educational dance.* London: Kimpton.

Redfern, H.B. (1975) The justification of dance as a curriculum activity, social and aesthetic aspects. Dunfermline College of P.E. *Journal of Psycho-social Aspects*, April, pp. 14-29.

Schools Council (1975) *Arts and the adolescent,* Working paper 54. London: Evans/Methuen.

CHAPTER III

Dance in the changing educational context of the 1970s

1
Changes in the teacher education context

2
The nature and structure of awards in 1973

3
The nature and structure of awards in 1976

4
Issues arising from changes in validation

In Chapter III current practical concerns are presented based on facts about dance in higher education which are not available elsewhere. From current practice problem areas, misconceptions, significant trends etc. are identified and in this way a link is made between Chapters II and IV. However, if readers wish to proceed immediately to theoretical issues they should move straight to Chapter IV.

Structures for the study of dance were in existence, albeit in an embryonic form, in the early 1970s. For reasons already given the higher education sphere is the sector from which information is derived. It serves as an example. In addition, the teacher education part of it has a crucial role to play in training the next generation of dance teachers. In performing this role it determines, to a substantial extent, the nature and content of the dance curriculum in schools.

Within the state education sector dance faced serious problems in the 1970s when teacher education went through a period of reorganisation. Changes in the status and organisation of institutions and in the structure and nature of awards offered were combined with a drastic reduction in the number of teacher education places allocated to colleges. Hence pressures on all subjects in the college of education curriculum.

The consequences and implications for dance of the restructuring of the non-university higher education system are considered here under three headings:

1. changes in the teacher education context
2. changes in the nature and structure of awards
3. issues arising from changes in validation.

Some of the information presented here is derived from sources generally available (e.g. the James Report and the White Paper) and the purpose of the summary is to give a broad framework since changes in dance may arise not only from within the subject but also in response to external pressures. The specific information pertaining to the study of dance was obtained from an investigation into the nature, purpose and structure of dance courses in existence between 1973 and 1980 in 40 institutions of higher education. The full details of the methodology, institutions involved etc. are given in the thesis which resulted (Adshead, 1980) but main facts and major outcomes are included because they inform the ensuing discussion.

Since dance existed principally in the teacher education system, the majority of the 40 institutions selected were (in 1975) concerned almost solely with initial teacher education. The 33 colleges of education were selected from approximately 170 such institutions in existence at that time in England, Wales and Scotland. However, in order to encompass the range of types of institution in which dance could be studied and to make comparisons, three colleges of the arts, out of eight in total in England, Wales and Scotland, were selected. Dartington College of Arts, the Laban Centre for Movement and Dance and the London College of Dance and Drama were approached because of their emphasis on dance and because they had established links with the state sector so that their students could become qualified teachers. In addition, four universities where dance may be part of an undergraduate or postgraduate course of study, as distinct from a recreative or extra curricula activity, were included. These were the universities of Birmingham, Hull, Leeds and Manchester. A complete list of the institutions involved may be found in Appendix A.

By means of questionnaires, interviews with tutors responsible for dance, and analysis of course submissions, information was derived concerning, for example, the changing status of institutions; the structure of awards; the nature of the dance taught; the content of courses and the amount of time available for dance in different awards.

1. Changes in the teacher education context

While the changes described here affect the whole of the

teacher education curriculum it is clear that dance, as a subject of study in this context, was at the same time at a stage of development where external pressures might have considerable effects. In this case, internal developments in dance, described in the previous chapter, seem to have been accelerated by these pressures.

The underlying external issue in many respects has been the decline in the birth rate and hence the lower projections of the number of teachers required. It became clear in the late 1960s that supply would overtake demand in the unexpectedly near future, assuming other factors remained constant, for example, pupil-teacher ratios. Although initially the lower number of places needed was seen as an opportunity to improve the standard of entrants to teacher training and the quality of the courses offered this ideal was limited by unforeseen economic problems. The reduction of student places, combined with pressures for economies which supposedly derive from larger institutions, has resulted in the cessation of initial training in approximately one third of colleges. In consequence some colleges closed entirely while others sought survival by merging with similar institutions or with further education colleges or polytechnics.

Related to these pressures for change was a further one, the development in the 1960s of the binary system of higher education and apparent governmental preference for expansion outside the university sector. Reasons for this included the growing number of school leavers qualified for, and desiring, entry to higher education and the perceived greater accountability and social responsiveness of the polytechnics and colleges of further education. The Area Training Organisation (A.T.O.) system which had linked the colleges of education to universities was disbanded following the James report thus severing the formal connections between many colleges and universities. The move towards the non-university sector of higher education is clearly revealed in the colleges sampled.

The reorganisation of the 33 colleges of education sampled in this study has resulted in 7 remaining free standing with a substantial commitment to teacher education, 8 merging with one or more colleges of further and/or higher education, 9 merging with polytechnics, 5 federating with one or more other colleges and 4 associating or affiliating with a university or polytechnic. These mergers and federations, combined with a drastic reduction in teacher education places which averaged 33% over the country as a whole, have imposed structural changes on institutions which affect the place of dance.

To achieve viability within prevailing notions of economies of scale and size there has been a reconsideration of subject boundaries and of the relationship between subjects. Since dance had no existence as a subject in its own right *apart* from its teacher education context (therefore no fixed boundaries or recourse to university knowledge structures) it was particularly vulnerable to change.

In order to determine the place of dance in the reorganised institutions college tutors were asked where dance was located, i.e. within which department or faculty, and whether this had changed between 1973 and 1976. The results are given below.

Table 1: The place of dance in the sampled institutions

Dept. or Faculty in which dance was located	No. of institutions	
	1973	1976
Arts	0	8
Dance	13	4
Drama	1	1
Human movement studies	0	9
Movement, music, drama	1	1
Movement studies	4	2
Physical Education	18	9
Theatre	1	1
Total	38	35

N.B. 1. The lower total in 1976 reflects institutional mergers.
    2. Total 1973 = 38 + 2 dance colleges = 40.

The Arts category includes 'School of Visual and Performing Arts', 'Humanities and Performing Arts', 'Faculty of Fine Art and Design', 'Faculty of Education and the Performing Arts' and 'Creative Arts', while one Arts department subsumes movement studies. Within the Human Movement Studies category (H.M.S.), departmental titles include 'Human Movement Studies, Sport and Recreation', 'School of Human Movement and P.E.' and 'Human Movement', while one department is subsumed under the 'Faculty of Social Sciences' and one under the 'Faculty of Education and Social Studies'.

It is clear from these figures that it is now less usual to find dance under the aegis of P.E. or as a department in its own right and that it is just as likely to be found under H.M.S. or the Arts. It could be argued that a H.M.S. department amounts to the same orientation as a P.E. department but respondents claimed that this is not the case. The crucial factor is seen to be the change of emphasis from the professional context in which physical activities have usually occurred (i.e. in education), to the study of human movement in its own right.

It would appear that some of the colleges which had a separate dance department in 1973 have been forced by the pressures of amalgamation and reduction in student numbers to merge with other departments. Most of these departments re-emerge as part of Arts departments. The remaining few, often in former specialist P.E. colleges, have lost their independent status and returned to the P.E. or H.M.S. area for reasons of viability.

The interviewer, who visited all the institutions in the sample, followed up the question of the location of dance by asking for the reasons for such changes. While most respondents stated that in an ideal world dance would be found in a department of its own or within an arts department (preferably performing or creative arts) they had been unable to achieve this. The reasons are summarised here through typical quotations.

1. *'No institution starts with a clean slate', they have had to be pragmatic and work within existing structures, the end result is 'an uneasy compromise between ideals and viability factors'.*

2. *In some cases the 'strength of the institutions was in training specialist teachers of P.E.' and the survival of the college was seen to depend on continuing to offer this specialism. Given the reduction in student numbers it was 'not possible to specialise further, if anything, less', hence the disappearance of some dance departments into H.M.S.*

3. *'The links with P.E. have proved valuable', 'dance has much to offer P.E. and H.M.S.', 'as long as students experience dance it does not matter under which umbrella', 'H.M.S. without the aesthetic would be incomplete'. 'To remove dance from P.E. would make justifying P.E. more difficult', and that 'other aspects of P.E. have a minority appeal to girls'. The college emphasis on movement and ways of classifying it leads to dance 'finding a natural home in movement studies'.*

4. *'Arts aims are consistent with aims in dance' and conversely, that 'the behavioural objectives emphasis within the Social Sciences (under which H.M.S. is sometimes subsumed) are inconsistent', leading to 'problems in identifying and evaluating aims in dance'.*

5. *Dance has had an 'uneven development' mainly in education, and until courses 'have broadened and the subject is seen as worthy of study in its own right in higher education', the situation is not likely to change.*

6. *Concern was expressed about possible career outlets for dance students (as distinct from P.E. students who do some dance) and staff were reluctant to educate for unspecified outcomes.*

The gradual clarification of dance study described in Chapter II and the consequent emphasis on its art form aspects in the context of aesthetic education would appear to have had a strong influence on the views expressed by dance tutors.

Ideals, though, are limited by practical realities. Although there is acknowledgement of the strengths as well as the weaknesses of a connection with Physical Education, the growth of Human Movement Studies and clarification of areas of academic study distinct from the practical application in Physical Education has released dance from too close a dependence on the area.

However, because of the reduction in the number of teacher education places required and the resulting institutional and departmental mergers there have been constraints on this desire for a separate existence. In consequence dance has not been able to 'strike out' independently in most cases but has either maintained a link with P.E. or H.M.S., if that was its place before, or joined forces with other arts subjects if it was, in 1975, a separate department.

2. The nature and structure of awards in 1973

The three year Certificate of Education course was originally the only course offered in higher education institutions (with the exception of the arts colleges and private institutions) which included dance. It was primarily a qualification to teach and secondarily a subject qualification. In the former specialist P.E. colleges there was a much greater subject emphasis and training to teach was limited to the secondary age range. In the mid 1960s a fourth year B.Ed. course, in which dance could be studied, was made available in some institutions.

While some would argue that the main subject studied in a college of education course had nothing to do with teaching and consisted of the study of the subject for its own sake it seems clear that dance, as a 'subject' for its own sake where it did occur was in no viable sense an equivalent in stature, literature, complexity or standard to music or other arts subjects. In only twenty out of 170 colleges was it even a separate subject from P.E.

Few students studied dance at the depth even of a main level course, although within some specialist P.E. courses an equivalent depth of study was possible. All students training to be teachers were likely to follow a brief P.E. method course to prepare them to teach P.E. in the primary school which would probably include a few hours dance or 'movement'. The numbers of students involved in some kind of dance study within a main dance or P.E. or advanced P.E. course in the institutions sampled are given in Table 2.

Table 2: The number of students commencing dance courses in 1973 on the three year certificate of education in sampled institutions

Type of course	Number of courses	Number of students on each course	
		range	mean
Main dance	14	4 - 23	15
Main P.E.	14	12 - 70	25
Advanced P.E.	17	30 - 180	79

It is clear from these figures that the numbers of students involved in main level dance courses was so few that under pressure of the reduction of teacher education places some courses would cease to exist. It is also obvious that the colleges offering advanced P.E. courses (notably the former specialist colleges) would have much greater flexibility and potential for the survival of the subject than would the colleges offering main level dance courses. This is an ironic situation since the P.E. connection had in some instances inhibited the development of artistic considerations in dance study.

The following diagram gives the number of hours of dance study available both in compulsory and optional courses in 1973 in the sampled colleges.

It is immediately obvious, for example, that the label 'main P.E.' of itself meant little and that the possibilities for dance study varied within it enormously. Generalisations are difficult

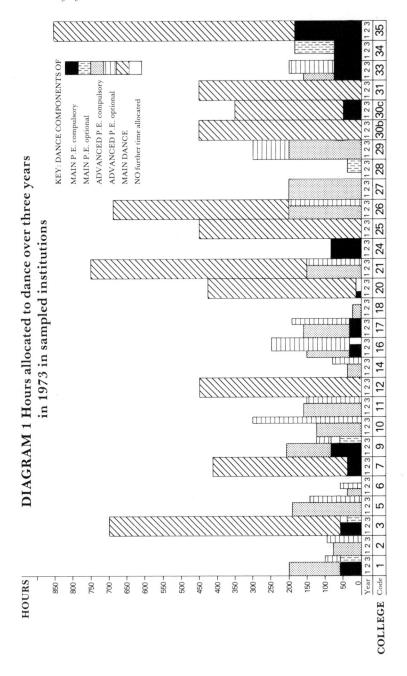

DIAGRAM 1 Hours allocated to dance over three years in 1973 in sampled institutions

to make, the only sound one being obvious, that a main dance course offered a longer study of the subject than a main P.E. course. The detail is, nonetheless, of interest since some colleges offered so little dance that it hardly appears on the diagram and, as might be anticipated, these are the men's colleges or those colleges offering a mixed P.E. course. The hours given on the diagram do not, in most cases, include the 'method' or professional studies component of dance study, i.e. the preparation of students for teaching. This information may be found in Table 3.

Table 3: Number of hours allocated to dance on curriculum courses in 1973

Type of course	No. of courses	Compulsory/ optional	Range of time allocation in hours	Mean time allocation in hours
Training for	10	compulsory	4 - 50	24
Primary Schools	4	option	10 - 60	27
Training for	3	compulsory	5 - 36	17
Middle Schools	2	option	10 - 30	20
Training for	8	compulsory	10 - 60	24
Infant, Junior &	3	option	10 - 30	17
Secondary Schools				
Specialist dance course, training for all age ranges	3	compulsory	100	100
Specialist P.E.	7	compulsory	12 - 50	29
course, students	1	option	40	
training for	7		within dance time—	
Secondary Schools			hours unspecified	
Training for a broad age range (Post graduate Certificate of Education)	10	compulsory for some students	7 - 60	26

(Left margin labels: Three Year — Certificate of Education for the first six course groups; One Year for the final course group.)

Professional, curriculum or method courses in the institutions in the survey were varied, both in structure and time allocated.

In examining these curriculum courses the adequacy of the preparation for teaching might be questioned. The majority of students undertaking courses for teaching in primary and middle schools would have an average dance allocation of 20 hours. Since they would not, in general, be taking main or advanced level dance or P.E. courses this 20 hours involved the students in learning about the activity (with little previous personal dance experience) in addition to learning how to teach it. Students following specialist dance and P.E. courses were offered a greater amount of time in preparation for teaching.

The fourth year B.Ed. course in the old system had allowed students in some institutions to spend half their time on dance study (10 of the sampled colleges). Alternatively dance could form part of the study of P.E. in varying amounts (12 of the colleges) while in 20 institutions it was not possible to pursue study in dance beyond the Certificate level although a B.Ed. in P.E. was offered. Some colleges offered courses in more than one of these categories.

3. The nature and structure of awards in 1976

Following the James report and the White Paper, changes in the structure of awards were made enabling a student to take a B.Ed. degree at Ordinary level after three years or at Honours level after four years, each award embodying a teaching qualification. In turn this affected the content and structure of courses, the traditional concurrent course for teacher training becoming consecutive in some colleges and the established pattern of a three part structure of education, a main subject and professional studies altering in diverse ways. In the interest of co-ordinating the training and induction process more meaningfully students were to undergo an induction year and teacher tutors were to be appointed in schools. The implementation of these latter plans has, however, been limited by the economic situation.

In addition new courses (called 'diversified courses' since they were not concerned with the training of teachers) have emerged in order that institutions might attract viable numbers of students. In Table 4 which illustrates the range of awards dance components may range from a small to a substantial part of courses with these titles.

Table 4: New course patterns in 1976

3 year B.Ed. (Ordinary)	4 year B.Ed. (Honours)	— *dance teaching qualification*

2 year Diploma of Higher Education Dip.H.E.

1/2 year M.A. M.Phil. M.Ed. → 3 year Ph.D. research

3 year Ordinary degree B.A. Performing Arts/ Fine Arts B. Combined Studies B. Human Movement Studies B. Humanities

3/4 year Honours degree B.A. B. Combined Studies B. Human Movement Studies B.A. Dance

non-vocational dance courses

1 year postgraduate certificate of education (P.G.C.E.) ——— *dance teaching qualification*

45

The new B.Ed. degrees came into being between 1967 and 1980, the peak year for commencement being 1975-6. The fact of having students with potentially different career intentions in one institution (i.e. intending teachers and those following diversified courses) exerted pressure on the structure of the curriculum since courses have to have a minimum number of students in order to be viable. Hence the separation of teacher education elements from subject study. Combined with a move towards greater student choice of courses these factors have led in many cases to the restructuring of the curriculum on a module or unit basis. This is a new approach and one with significant implications for dance. The greater flexibility of structure is evident in Table 5, since teacher training components are separate from subject study and, in theory, the subject units could contribute to other degrees.

There are a number of points that are of interest arising from Table 5. The first is the diversity of structure which now exists. It proved impossible to reduce the rather formidable set of tables to a smaller number since each institution has a different kind of course. While even a 'unit' of study varies between 40 and 300 hours the *proportion* of time allocated respectively to education and to subject study within the B.Ed. degree remains fairly constant. Time is most frequently divided equally although some colleges allow more time for subject study than they allow for education and some allow less. It is not necessarily the case that the colleges which allocate more time to subject study train secondary school teachers although one might expect it to be.

Thus the balance of studies which is seen to be appropriate for intending teachers who also have degrees is one area of interest. Within the subject time it is possible to trace differing patterns of compulsory and optional courses in dance within the predominant H.M.S. subject area. Relatively few colleges link dance with drama and other arts subjects although the tendency increases in degrees which are not oriented towards teaching.

The teaching studies column reveals disparate provision and illustrates the difficulty of making a clear statement since dance is often included in unspecified amounts within a broadly based unit.

The diversification of colleges from a purely teacher education role to a broader base is illustrated by the development of new courses in institutions sampled in the study. By 1978 there were ten new B.A. non-teaching degrees in which dance might be studied, two Performance/Creative arts degrees, one B.A. Theatre, one B.A. in Dance, and four Dip.H.E. courses. At the same time a further 16 courses were in the process of validation.

While it might be a sound development for dance that it should appear in a range of awards the pressures have come both from the need to make courses viable by attracting students who are not training to teach and from the art orientation. Viability is often achieved by students taking general higher education courses being taught together with those intending to be teachers for specified periods of the course.

A further structural development is clear. The organisation of study into units allows greater student choice and gives flexibility so that students with different career intentions may follow some of the same courses. Again in the search for viability subjects may be grouped together and the development of interdisciplinary studies exemplifies this trend, e.g. Creative Arts.

B.A. courses which demand the study of more than one art and which include dance appear under a range of titles, for example, Expressive arts, Creative arts, Performing and Performance arts. As their titles indicate, there are unifying notions underlying these courses, frequently revealed by core components concerning the concept of 'art', methods employed by artists across a range of media, a study of the creative process, the arts in society, etc. For example, one B.A. Performance arts (3 year Ord. or Hons.) is structured around a

Table 5: The structure of three year B. Ed. Ord. and four year

Inst. Code	No. of Units B.Ed.Ord.	Hons.	Structure				
1	54		Ed : T. studies : Prac. T. : Special subject				
			17	10	10	17	3 yr units Ord.
			375		150	300	4th yr hrs. Hons.
2	34	44	Ed : Prof. st. : Prac. T. : H.M.S.				
			6	5	3	18	3 yr Ord.
			+ 2 options Ed/H.M.S.				
			6			4	4th yr Hons.
					or		
			4			6	
3	9 plus special exercise	12	Ed : Teaching : Subject study				3 yr Ord.
			5	1		3	
			1			2	4th yr Hons.
5	18	21	Ed : Prof. st. : T.P. : P.E.				
			4½	5	3	4½	3 yr Ord.
			+ 1 supplementary				
			1½			1½	4th yr Hons.

KEY

	Comp. St.	— Complementary studies
	H.M.S.	— Human movement studies
	Mvt.	— Movement
Ed. — Education	P.E.	— Physical education

B. Ed. Hons. courses in dance in 1976 in the sampled institutions

	Dance Components		Teaching Studies	1 Unit =
Year I	Mvt. st. includes prac. dance & aesthetics	5 units	Mvt. studies 2 units	45 hrs.
Year II	Mvt. st. *or* Art of mvt.	5 units		
Year III	Mvt. st *or* Art of mvt.	7 units		
Year IV	Mvt. st. (no Art of mvt.) includes	300 hrs		
	Aesthetics option Special study	35 hrs		
Year I-III	H.M.S. core & options		H.M.S. 4 units	45 hrs.
	Theory	5/6 units		
	Practical includes dance	8/10 units		
Year IV	Arts aspects option	2 units		
Year I	H.M.S. includes prac. dance and theoretical studies	1 unit	Curriculum theory and practice	200 hrs.
Year II	Mvt. as a medium for expression and communication	1 unit	2 units includes dance	
Year III	Dance composition	1 unit		
Year IV	H.M.S. perspectives includes dance	1 unit		
Year I	Foundation P.E. includes dance		Profess. linked to practical studies	54 hrs.
Year II & III	Two from three options—one philos. & aesthetic		Year I 50 Hrs. Year II 40 Hrs.	
Year IV—	cont. study of one plus dissertation		plus options	

Prac. T.	— Practical teaching		Sec.	— Secondary
T.P.	— Teaching practice		Sub.	— Subject
Prof. St.	— Professional studies		T. St.	— Teaching studies
Sch.	— School		Inst. Code	— Institution code number

Inst. Code	No. of Units B.Ed.Ord.	Hons.	Structure
6	12	16	Ed & Prof. st. : T.P. : Subjects 4 min 2 min 3 yr Ord. 6 min 4 min 4th yr Hons. + link study
7	18	24	Ed : T. studies : T.P. : Subjects 4 3 3 8 3 yr units 2 4 4th yr units

9	9	12	Ed & applied st. : T.P. : Subject
			5 Term 8 4 3 yr Ord.
			                               Sec. Spec.
			                               P.E.
			6 3 Junior
			7 2 Infant
			1 + 1 1 4th yr Hons.

10	3 yr Dip. 12	4 yr Ord. Hons. 17	Ed : T.P. : Mvt. st. : Comp. st. 220 9 400 240 2 yrs. hrs. wks. hrs. 3 4 2 Dip. yr 3 4 5 2 4th yr Ord. Hons.
11			1978 changes in organisational status, further restructuri
12 & 26	9 at least	12	Ed : Profess. st. : T.P. : Main subject 2-3 2-3 1½ 4 3 yr course 1 min 2 min 4th yr

Dance Components			Teaching Studies	1 Unit =
ear I-III	Dance units available, linked with drama and movement	3 units	Drama and dance in the primary school 1 unit P.E. method includes dance 15 hrs.	90 hrs.
ear IV	Dance as an art form	1 unit		
ear I, II, III	min 4, max 8 courses in any one course area max 5 dance courses (units)		Mvt. studies 1 unit Dance, secondary 1 unit First/middle school includes some dance 3 units	90 hrs.
ear IV	min 3 in subject area			
ear I	Foundation course H.M.S. includes dance	1 unit	P.E. & Dance within Ed. & applied studies units 1 unit	300 hrs.
ear II	Choice of 2 perspectives, one may be dance as an art form	1 unit		
ear III	Dance in Ed. in relation to H.M.S. choice (sec. only)	1 unit		
ear IV	Continuing study of 2 perspectives	1 unit		
ear I & II	Basic course Mvt. st. includes dance, approx. one-fifth			150 hrs.
ear III & IV	Option, all mvt. st. time, dance			
courses anticipated				
Main subject, *either* Mvt. st. (P.E.) including some dance *or* Mvt. st. (Art of Movement) 'A' & 'B' level units 'B's for Hons.			Ed. theory + practice min 5½ units secondary teaching, 6½ units primary	150 hrs.

Inst. Code	No. of Units B.Ed.Ord.	Hons.	Structure
14	4 yr Ord. or Hons.		Ed : Academic : Practical P.E. studies P.E. studies 26% 37% 37% Ord. 41% 33% Hons.
15			Ed : Movement & Dance
16	24	32	Ed : Profess. st. : T.P. : Subject study 3½ 1 11½ Yr 1 & 2 4½ 3½ Yr 3 Ord. 3/4/5 3½ 3½ 3/4/5 Yr 3 & 4 Hons.
17	18	24	Ed : Profess. st. : T.P. : Subject areas 2 or 3 9 6 3 9 3 yr Ord. either 6 0 0 ⎫ or 3 3 0 ⎬ 4th yr or 3 3 ⎭ Hons. or 3 3
18	36	43	Ed : Profess. st. : T.P. : Major Sub. 3 9 2 16 Minor Sub. 3 yr 6 Ord. Major Sub. 2/3/4 2/3/4 4th yr + Link study 1/2 Hons.

Dance Components		Teaching Studies	1 Unit =
Year I & II Compulsory dance	1 unit	Profess. studies: dance included in 50 hour component in P.E.	40 hrs.
Year III & IV Options dance & aesthetics	1½ units yr 3 1½ units yr 4		
Two year course of 6 units followed by one or two year Ord./Hons. at 12			
Year I & II Dance pathway—		Dance route 1½ units P.E. route 1½ units includes dance	50 hrs.
dance	3 units		
related arts	3½ units		
H.M.S.	1 unit		
+ 2/3 other units			
H.M.S. pathway—			
compulsory dance	2 units		
option	1 unit		
Year III, IV Hons 3/4/5 courses each in 2 areas, e.g. H.M.S. & Arts ratio 6:3 or 5:4			
2, 3 or 6 unit H.M.S. courses for Ord. 9 or 12 unit H.M.S. courses for Hons.		Subject method 3 units	90 hrs.
Year I Foundation H.M.S.	2 units		
Option (dance)	1 unit		
Year II Core H.M.S.	1 unit		
Option (dance)	2 units		
Year III Profess.			
Year IV Art of Mvt. option	3 units		
Related profess. st.	3 units		
P.E. as major or minor subject	16/3 units	Dance method option 60 hrs.	50 hrs.
compulsory dance	30 hrs.		
options	30, 60, 120 hrs.		
aesthetics option	50 hrs.		

Inst. Code	No. of Units B.Ed.Ord.	Hons.	Structure
20	6	8	Ed : T. st. : T.P. : Subjects (2) 3 3 + 2 Hons.
21	56	66	Ed : T.P. : P.E. : Second sub. 16 20 16 3 yr Ord. 15 wks. concurrent + 4 free floating 5 5 4th yr Hons.
24	9	12	Ed : T.P. : Profess. st. : Main sub. 3 3/4 2/3 3yr Ord. 1 1 1 4th yr

25			Ed : T. st. : Subjects
			                 3yr Ord.
			                 4th yr Hons.

27	12	16	Ed : Profess. st. & T.P. : Subjects
			2 4 4 3 yr Ord.
			   + 2 electives
			2 1 4th yr Hons.
			   + 1 elective

28			No significant study of dance available

Dance Components		Teaching Studies	1 Unit =
Year I & II Dance units	2 units	Within P.E.	150 hrs.
Year III Profess. st. & T.P.		& arts	
Year IV Dance unit	1 unit	year III	
Year I Foundation P.E.		Profess. st.	27 hrs.
includes dance,	4 units	P.E.,	
then options		includes	
Year II & III Core units in		dance	
dance per yr	4 units	or Dance	
available +		3 units	
supplementary up to	6 units		
Year IV Either P.E. or Dance	5 units		
i.e. variable amounts from a little to dance			
& ed. solely			
Year I Foundation H.M.S.		P.E. compuls.	180 hrs.
includes dance		includes	
Year I, II & III Options up to	120 hrs.	dance 35 hrs.	
Year IV Skills or Dance	60 hrs.	Option for sec	
		30/60 hrs.	
Dance pathway possible		Dance in	96 hrs.
Year I	4 units	primary sch.	
Year II	4 units	$\frac{1}{3}$ unit	
Year III	Profess.	Teaching of	
Year IV	4 units	Dance & Mvt.	
		$\frac{1}{3}$ unit	
		Modern Ed.	
		Dance	
		$\frac{1}{3}$ unit	
4/5/6 unit P.E. courses		P.E. includes	120 hrs.
Year I & II Compulsory Dance	50 hrs	dance 20 hrs.	
Year III Option	46 hrs.	Year III option	
		Creative arts	
		includes dance	
		60 hrs.	
		P.E. includes	
		option in	
		dance 10 hrs.	

Inst. Code	No. of Units B.Ed.Ord.	Hons.	Structure
29	36	48	Ed : Profess. st. : T.P. : Main subjects (2) 8/11 14/16 14/21 Ord./Hon *Primary* 8/11 10/12 18/25 *Secondary*
30	10½ min	13½ min	Ed & Profess. st. : T.P. : Subjects or ed. 5 1½ 4 3 yr Ord. 1st & middle school 4 1½ 5 Secondary 3 4th yr now being renegotiated Hons.
31	12	16	Ed : Subjects 6/9 6/3 3 yr Ord. 2/3 2/1 4th yr Hon
33			Still under negotiation
34			Foundation : Major Ac. : Minor Ac. 25% 50% 25% Part I Profess. St. 50% 50% Part II B. Ed. Ord 4 3 4th yr B. Ed. Hon 3 4
35	27	36	Ed : Profess. st. : T.P. : Subjects 5 12 2 3 + 3 ⎫ 3 yr or ⎬ Ord. 5 + 1 ⎭ Primary + 2 options 5 8 2 7 + 2 Sec. + 2 options 3 individual project 3 3 4th yr Hons.

Dance Components		Teaching Studies	1 Unit =
Primary : 6 units per subject, core Sec. : 8 units per subject, core Dance units possible over 4 yrs	7 units	Primary: P.E. & Expressive Arts 2 ½ units Sec.: P.E. 6 units	50 hrs.

Year I   Compulsory core P.E.
   includes dance or totally
   Art of Mvt.
Year II & III   Up to 2 units
   art of mvt.
Year IV   Dance option
   link study
	1 ½ units
	
	1 unit
	½ unit
		1st & middle
		school mvt.
		studies 1 unit
		includes
		8 hrs. dance
		Secondary mvt.
		studies 1 unit
		includes 15 hrs
		dance Middle
		school elective
		½ unit
			150 hrs.

Year I-III units per year no hons. dance	1 ½ units	Primary: P.E. includes dance 20 hrs.	100 hrs.

Part I   Major study H.M.
  Compuls. aesthetics
   & philos.
   dance
  Option dance
Part II   Ord. H.M.
  Compuls. dance
  Option
Year IV   Hons. H.M.
  Compuls. philos. & H.M.
  Option dance
  Special study
	5 units
	50 hrs.
	48 hrs.
	96 hrs.
	3 units
	21 hrs.
	54 hrs.
	3/4 units
	1 unit
	2 units
	1 unit
		P.E. 1 unit	60 hrs.

Dance as major or minor component Year I 3 units Year II 2/4/5 units Year IV 3 units	i.e. 3/5/7/10 unit dance course	Expressive Arts includes dance 2 units Dance 1 unit	60 hrs.

first study, either of dance or drama or music (time allocation approximately 1,100 hours); core studies which focus on the idea of 'performance' where the arts are presented as interrelated; supporting studies in arts other than that chosen for the first study; and performance projects. The Honours element consists of a special exercise. The aims of this course might be summarised as to achieve understanding in the arts, combined with a high level of individual performance in one, within the context of projects which combine the arts. The key concept here is of interrelationship between the arts.

A second B.A. of this type involves students in participation in three arts (dance, drama and music) equally during the first year in order to 'examine and experience the techniques necessary for the creative act of performing', before requiring specialisation in subsequent years. 'Conceptual' studies of, for example, the notions of 'communication' and 'creativity', and 'interaction' studies relating the media involved indicates the general approach of this course to the performing arts. In contrast to the previously described course, this one requires fieldwork in the community and a personal project or dissertation. All students study for a three year Honours degree.

A B.A. Theatre degree, which is a four year Honours course, has a 'sandwich' element of a full year, the third, spent working in the community, for example, with travelling theatre groups in remote rural areas. 'Central studies' of acting, writing, and moving form the core of the course. In the first instance the emphasis of the movement work is on 'release' studies, an anatomically based movement approach which is developed in later years into contemporary dance styles and choreography. It is possible in this B.A. course to pursue a study of dance in some depth, but on the whole the movement/dance element is seen as servicing other aspects of the course. However, this internationally known college of the arts attracts experts in unusual areas of dance, and such options as the dance of Japan and India give a broader cultural approach than that of other courses analysed.

B.A. Combined studies degrees allow an institution to offer a wide range of subjects in combination. It is usual to expect a student to study two subjects in depth, and, as an example of some of the combinations available, the University of London* offers through its constituent colleges, the possibility of studying dance with music, religion, English and drama, philosophy, history etc. In this case the subjects studies are discrete areas of knowledge and are each allocated half the available time.

The first B.A. (Hons) purely in dance was validated during the period of this study in a sampled college and the first intake of students commenced in 1976. It is a three year full time course on a core studies with options pattern. Required studies over the duration of the course are in the areas of dance technique, choreography, movement studies (including notation) and aesthetics. Components in history of dance (compulsory over two years), visual arts, drama and music (over four terms) are pursued for shorter periods and a system of options allows depth study in one of the following; history of dance, dance and society, music accompaniment or composition for dance, notation or production.

A number of B.A. in Human Movement (H.M.S.) degrees have been proposed but few with dance elements are yet in operation. Courses vary fundamentally in approach, some proceeding from the academic study of the disciplines of psychology, sociology and philosophy, and others from the activities themselves, with supporting academic studies.

4. Issues arising from changes in validation

Any award offered by the public or private sector of education is subject to some kind of ratification procedure. Public criteria are necessarily required in order that standards of awards are consistent, from C.S.E. to private dancing school awards, e.g.

*London University is to cease validation by 1983

of the I.S.T.D. etc. The issues raised here are common to all awards at all levels but the example which illustrates this is taken from the state higher education system.

In the former colleges of education prior to the reorganisation public scrutiny took the form of close attention to examination papers and practical examinations etc. through examiners appointed by the body ultimately responsible (in this case the universities). Some attention was given to the structure and content of courses through subject boards but, on the whole, syllabi and content evolved through general academic interchange and the only public statement for dance in the state education sector was a few lines in a hand-book of courses, rather than detailed course submissions.

There are of course wider issues here of how far the class teacher should be autonomous and how far outside agencies should control the process.

Two of the far reaching implications of the White Paper were that many institutions would (a) seek to offer new awards of a diversified type and (b) would restructure the Certificate course in order to offer a three year B.Ed. degree (Ord.) and a four year Honours degree. Because of institutional amalgamations with non-university colleges and polytechnics, and the general reluctance of universities to get involved in validating college degrees that were not teacher education based, the Council for National Academic Awards (C.N.A.A.) emerged as an important route to viability. Of course, polytechnics already had degrees validated by the C.N.A.A. and the machinery was well established, thus a college which became part of a polytechnic would logically cease its association with the university. Other colleges thought (not always wisely as it turned out) that it would be an easier and quicker route to developing new courses than the supposedly ponderous university machinery since the sole purpose of the C.N.A.A.'s existence is to validate awards. In some cases the long established relationship between a university and its colleges allowed innovation to take place relatively painlessly and quickly based on mutual respect. In other cases poor relationships hastened the move to C.N.A.A. In some universities there had been a refusal to validate dance at B.Ed. Hons. level (when the possibility arose following the Robbins report) although P.E. was seen to be acceptable. In at least one institution this reluctance provided a spur to entering into negotiations with the C.N.A.A.

While it is taken for granted that it is a good thing that 'standards' should be maintained it is not so easy to be explicit about what constitutes a 'good' course, since criteria may be diverse and conflicting. The notion of what constitutes a 'degree' has many interpretations in the U.K. and even wider ones in the U.S.A. which stretch the boundaries of the concept. Much opposition has resulted, some from a position of entrenched prejudice, for example, taking the view that only one of the traditionally established forms of knowledge studied for its own sake is appropriate for the award of a degree, some of genuine concern for the standard of work of an intellectual kind that is possible (or not possible) in a degree which combines several subjects or which is also concerned with practical work or which applies knowledge to a work context.

Particular problems are posed for dance because it is centrally a practical activity and arguments range from one extreme of saying that practical participation in dance has nothing to do with a degree (if the notion of a degree is of intellectual activity) to the opposite view that practical involvement in dancing is what dance is about and is the only central component.

Problems of comparability have always arisen between science and arts based degrees since their verification procedures are so different. With the new performing arts courses further difficulties are evident, for example, how does one compare work in 'academic' subjects based on literary sources with that involving 'creativity', where technical skills must be learnt, not only for precision of expression but also for understanding and in order to produce a sufficiently high level of performance. Indeed is it possible to establish standards for creativity? In relation to course construction it is clear, from a study of files held at the C.N.A.A. concerning courses submitted to the Creative and Performing Arts Panel (Adshead, 1980) that one of the main difficulties is to find a suitable focus to hold multi-disciplinary studies together and to give them coherence. A core component is often seen to be the solution. A breadth of studies might be seen to militate against depth involvement, but this is a difficult balance since some width of grasp of a subject is clearly desirable and so also is the understanding which comes from investigation into a small part of it in depth. It is a further problem to find the appropriate balance between practical and theoretical work in relation to the aims of the course even assuming that the practical element can be justified in the first place.

Methods of evaluation in an arts curriculum are also problematic. If such a curriculum tends to be open-ended and speculative and, in Kaufman's terms:

> . . . *functions most effectively as it offers alternatives rather than prescriptions, counsel rather than exhortation, suggestive cues rather than directives, points from which to begin rather than points at which to end*

(in Eisner 1971 p.98)

then indeed evaluation/assessment is fraught with difficulties. There is a great need for research into assessment methods which are appropriate for the arts, which reflect the subject concerned, and yet record the learner's progress in under-standing, if only as feedback in the teaching situation.*

Some of the confusion about the place of dance in relation to P.E., H.M.S. and the Arts is reflected in the problems of validation. Before the new structures, most dance courses were within P.E. and validated by universities. Since, with few exceptions, universities had no staff with qualifications in P.E.

---

*See the Gulbenkian Foundation report: *Dance Education and Training in Britain,* 1980, Chapter 12.

the university representatives on these committees were most usually from other disciplines seen to be relevant to P.E., e.g. physiology. While this was a source of some friction for physical educationists it was even more so for dance staff in colleges since the expertise of university staff seemed remote from their concerns.

The differentiation between various aspects of P.E. and notably here the artistic emphasis in the dance area has posed problems in relation to validating bodies. For example, in 1968 the C.N.A.A. set up the Committee in Education with subject panels to advise it, including a panel for physical education. This panel was involved in validating B.Ed. degrees and Certificates in Education in which P.E. and/or dance played a part. The Combined Studies Board of the existing Committee for Arts and Social Studies acquired a Creative and Performing Arts panel in 1975 as a response to the changing needs of the validation process. This panel considered proposals for Dip.H.E. and B.A. awards which combined two or more arts. An additional board for Humanities (also under the Combined Studies Board) has also validated a degree in which dance had a place. Recently, the Committee for Arts and Social Studies has divided into the Committee for Arts and Humanities and the Committee for Business and Social Studies. The original P.E. panel changed its name to 'Movement studies' but has in 1979 reverted to the P.E. title after much discussion. At the same time a new Recreation and Sports Studies Board has been formed under the Arts and Humanities Committee. This presumably reflects the type of submissions which the C.N.A.A. has been receiving and, therefore, changes in the boundaries surrounding aspects of the subject.

The Committee for Arts and Social Studies, as it was then, created a Movement and Dance panel in 1976 to consider the first B.A. Dance proposal. As clarification of the roles of the various panels and board has taken place it has emerged that this panel, now called the Dance Board (i.e. upgrading and dropping the 'movement' label) is to deal with single subject awards in dance, as distinct from combined subject awards.

The Dance Board is composed of a group of people concerned with dance in the theatre and dance in education.

Dance is also represented in the C.N.A.A. validation structure on the P.E. panel of the Committee for Education (for B.Ed. courses) as well as on the boards illustrated below:

**COMMITTEE FOR ARTS
AND HUMANITIES**

Subject boards   Combined studies   Drama and Theatre   Dance   Recreation and Sports studies

Creative and Performing arts   Humanities

While individual validators cross reference between committees it is a reflection of recent debate that dance appears under so many umbrellas and has such different contexts. Does anything emerge from these different perspectives that could coherently use the same label 'dance'? This question is pursued in Chapter IV while the reader who has a greater interest in validation and the perception of college dance tutors might wish to consult Appendix B.

However, it is possible to draw together certain statements about course construction which give general guidelines. Criteria for course construction were identified from interview material and from research into the archives held at C.N.A.A.

Criteria

1. *Courses should be coherent and unified, with a common rationale guiding the total programme.*

   Factors militating against this are the complex structure of many programmes, the viability necessity of overlapping B.Ed. and diversified courses, the overloading of courses with subject material, and the nature of combined studies, e.g. performing arts.

2. *Courses should have breadth with a unifying overview but should also offer depth study; should have continuity and sequential progression.*
Difficulties in this area arise in determining how broad a range of topics can be covered without losing coherence; when and to what extent depth studies should be pursued; how studies in dance can be logically developed.

3. *Courses should have a sound conceptual basis and be intellectually demanding.*
Problems arise here in determining the focus of the course and its theoretical orientation; in deciding what constitutes honours degree work in dance, particularly in the context of combined or related subjects, and what content is appropriate for each year of study.

4. *Objectives must be related to aims and content.*
The fundamental debate here is whether academic objectives are complementary or integral or unrelated to performance objectives; of what is an acceptable standard of performance for different types of courses; of disentangling performance objectives from those of understanding in the arts.

The course criteria isolated during the study could provide a basis for considering existing and new course proposals were it not for the fact that the terms used by validators are open to many interpretations. For example, courses which are 'coherent and unified' would be universally commended but it is open to speculation what a unified or coherent course in dance would be like. Similarly breadth and depth are relative constructs.

Summary

Despite the many problems of the reorganisation of higher education in the 1970s it forced upon the dance education world a need to achieve greater clarity about the nature and purposes of an education in dance, particularly in terms of the *subject matter of dance* as distinct from *methodologies for teaching*. There is, however, evidence of considerable diversity and confusion in aims, content and evaluation and a coherent framework does not appear. (Details of current types of course content may be found in Adshead, 1980.) If the private sector of dance education is also taken into account then the diversity and confusion increases (see The Gulbenkian Foundation report *Dance Education and Training in Britain,* 1980). And yet it is *dance* which is being taught. There must be some consistency about what goes under this label, especially in terms of concepts and theories, even though the manifestations of dance which are taught may vary.

References and further reading

Adshead, J. (1980) Dance as a discipline. University of Leeds Ph.D. thesis.

Council for National Academic Awards. Charter and statutes; Annual reports.

D.E.S. (1972) *Teacher education and training.* Report by a Committee of inquiry under the chairmanship of Lord James of Rusholme. London: H.M.S.O.

D.E.S. (1972) *Education: a framework for expansion.* Command paper 5174. London: H.M.S.O.

Eisner, E.W. (1971) *Confronting curriculum reform.* Boston: Little, Brown.

Gulbenkian Foundation (1980) *Dance education and training in Britain.*

Lane, M. (1975) *Design for degrees.* London: MacMillan.

Lomax, D. (1973) (Ed.) *The education of teachers in Britain.* London: Wiley.

Parry, J.P. (1972) *The Lord James tricycle.* London: Allen and Unwin.

Raggett, M. and Clarkson, M. (1976) *Changing patterns of teacher education.* London: Falmer.

CHAPTER IV

Dance as a discipline: conceptual frameworks

1
Dance as 'movement', dance as 'art'

2
Basic tools

3
Central concepts

4
Methods of procedure and verification
of success

It is perhaps pertinent to draw together threads from preceding chapters in order to determine how far a basic framework for the study of dance had evolved by the late 1970s. On this foundation it is then possible to point to developments and clarifications which might give rise to a coherent structure and to ask if there exists a set of concepts through which any or all forms of dance might be examined *whenever* and *wherever* they exist.

1. Dance as 'movement', dance as 'art'

While a review of manuscripts on dance in the early 15th century asserted that there existed a 'very respectable body of theoretical and practical dance literature' (reported in Kinkeldy, 1929) this was of course within the narrow context of court dance at a particular period in history and, in addition, confined to a small geographical area. The theories which were offered were relevant to that context but, as cultures changed and new forms of dance emerged to supercede established forms, such theories became redundant.

The early classification of steps, e.g. by Arbeau, and the later developments of technical systems, are located within particular *forms* of dance, while the movement theorists embrace a wider range of *activities* than dance alone. The disciplines approach which was started by the early dance theorists and grew into H.M.S. or social/anthropological/ philosophical studies of dance, lays emphasis on other disciplines and does not necessarily inform the student about the structure of dance itself in any depth. Similarly, educational concerns, in the sense of an emphasis on the benefits to be derived by children in schools from taking part in dance, have focused on justifications for dance in relation to personality development, health, socialisation and aesthetic education. In all this, where is the dance and what is it like?

There is an obvious analogy here with music—it is possible to study music, its composition, interpretation and performance, for its own sake, within clearly articulated analytic and critical procedures without doing anthropology, or sociology of music etc. The kind of analytical study involved need not be 'dry' or boring although it is clearly a different kind of undertaking from dancing in a performance, attending dance performances for pleasure and from making a dance. In the long term it is more akin to the musicologist's trade and, it is contended, is absolutely essential for the development of dance studies.

Different types of dance have been taught in schools and colleges and while in practice it appears that one form is abandoned for another in rapid succession there is a need to attempt a global view in order that curriculum decisions might be taken in the full knowledge of the *many* manifestations of dance and in the light of central concepts which might guide study. A framework is required which allows for changing contexts and changing forms. This framework is not found in misty notions of the 'spirit' of dance but in common elements of all dances. It should be noted that this is not a mistaken search for 'essences' but an attempt to clarify what it is to *study dance* while allowing for the importance of the context in which it occurs and which to some extent determines its structure.*

To return to the evidence concerning the present (1975-80) state of dance in higher education it is pertinent to recall that the predominant orientation is towards dance in an artistic context instead of the 1950s and 1960s orientation towards child centred educational ideas. Within this broad approach, however, there are polarities which, for the purposes of this text, are characterised as *'dance as movement'* and *'dance as art'*.

---

*As an example of a useful characterisation Hanna (1979) compares the many definitional attempts from the starting point of dance as human behaviour and forms a 'researcher's abstraction' of the concept of dance as 1. purposeful, 2. intentionally rhythmical, 3. culturally patterned sequences of, 4a. non-verbal body movements which are, 4b. other than ordinary motor activities, 4c. the motion having inherent and aesthetic value.

The limitations of this definition are pointed out in a book review, *Journal of Human Movement Studies*, Vol. 6, No. 2, 1980 by John Whiting.

Neither of these provides a totally satisfactory account, they merely reflect contexts of dance in relation to other subjects and the pressures described in Chapter III for viability of courses.

To identify some dance as 'movement' and some as, by implication, 'not movement' might seem odd or illogical since there are undeniable connections between the two. Movement is self evidently the material of dance whether it occurs in an art context or not but it is vitally important to be clear about the fundamental orientations which these two approaches characterise because they control the studying process. They are based on quite different assumptions about the nature of dance and the proper methods for studying it. These different approaches also reinforce the instability of the subject since there are immediately two kinds of dance, thus shared central concepts are difficult to find.

The fundamental distinction between the two approaches is to be found in the different underlying sets of conceptual structures applied to the study of dance. Within the *dance as movement* orientation concepts from the behavioural sciences have become the background to study with philosophical aspects less well developed. Diagram 2 illustrates the development from the original 'movement' approach of the early 1960s to the more sophisticated 'human movement studies' model of the middle and late 1970s. This movement approach led to greater distinctions being made between the various disparate movement activities; consequently in the search for unity and a conceptual structure human movement studies took a disciplines stance.

Implicit in this is a general approach of behavioural objectives and measurable outcomes in an empirical sense. Even historical aspects, which might be more sympathetic towards dance, concern the development of the traditional physical activities of Western cultures particularly in the context of physical education.

The inadequacies of this approach rest on the fact that it proceeds through other disciplines and, therefore, dance is one

Diagram 2: The development of movement studies into Human Movement Studies and the 'dance as movement' concept

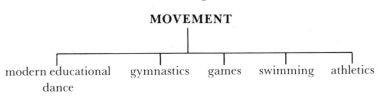

MOVEMENT

modern educational dance · gymnastics · games · swimming · athletics

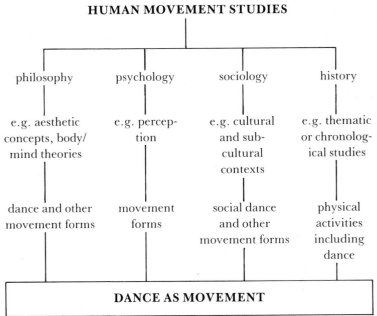

HUMAN MOVEMENT STUDIES

philosophy — e.g. aesthetic concepts, body/mind theories — dance and other movement forms

psychology — e.g. perception — movement forms

sociology — e.g. cultural and sub-cultural contexts — social dance and other movement forms

history — e.g. thematic or chronological studies — physical activities including dance

DANCE AS MOVEMENT

example among many of the possible movement forms. In addition it tends to ignore aesthetic concerns. In consequence there is little room for the development of conceptual structures around 'dance' since its nature can only be spelled out in psychological or social or historical terms.

The contrasted approach of the *dance as art* orientation has as its basis dance within a contextual framework of the development of an art form. Technique and choreographic studies

71

Diagram 3: The development of the study of dance and the 'dance as art' concept

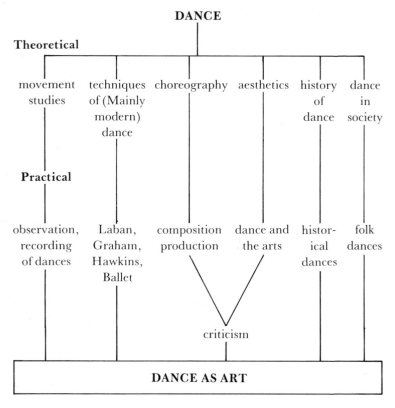

form the core and these usually relate to modern dance in the theatre (Diagram 3). While at least in this situation 'dance' rather than 'movement' is central, the embracing term 'dance' may be misleading since it is either explicitly or implicitly almost totally concerned with modern theatre dance and fails to take account of the many forms of dance. In other words, the dance as art approach is merely a summary of existing structures for courses with an art orientation and it does not therefore alone provide a satisfactory model for dance study in total. Nor would one expect it to.

The orientation of the study of dance towards either movement or art influences the aims and nature of dance courses, their progression and development, the teaching methods and evaluation procedures used. Confusion in the 'movement' orientation is manifest in course submissions and in the literature in the largely interchangeable use of the terms 'movement as expression' and 'dance as expression', and similarly, 'movement as communication' and 'dance as communication'. In these instances psychological states of the person are confounded with dance which communicates in a symbolic, artistic sense. As Best (1974) so clearly demonstrates, to study dance as an art is to consider it aesthetically, not empirically, and the movement orientation tends to draw it towards the empirical while the art orientation emphasises the aesthetic.

A further influence on the development of the concept of dance, this time from outside the education system, has been the emergence of a wide variety of movement-based fringe theatre forms in the 1970s. The boundaries of dance have become blurred in the process and what counts as dance covers a broader range of activity to the point where largely motionless activities or unstructured happenings involving movement of a gymnastic or athletic nature adopt the general label of dance.

In addition the development of a hitherto ill-defined area of study called variously 'Performing arts', 'Expressive arts' or 'Creative arts' which often includes dance is the result of closer relationships between art forms in the wider social context of the theatre and of developing studies in aesthetics which illuminate similarities and differences between such forms. It too, affects the orientation of dance studies since in this context the emphasis is often on creative projects involving more than one art. Substantial problems of organisation emerge in these areas of study and, more importantly, of setting aims and evaluating the outcomes of courses. Since courses in the performing arts tend to involve a depth study of one art, objectives related to standards of performance and understanding of the unique requirements of the particular form often come into conflict with the more generalised aims of interaction or integration in the arts.

It is already clear that the change towards an art orientation is not sufficient in itself for a coherent statement of the totality of dance study since it fails to take account of, for example, the movement-based fringe forms mentioned earlier as well as the examples of dance which are not art based. What is required is an approach or model which can encompass all these forms and which will allow for the study of past, present and future dance forms. Thus if 'dance' is qualified in specific instances by, for example, modern dance in the style of Graham's myth period or classical ballet in the style of Petipa, or tap dance in the style of Bojangles Robinson, what (if anything) remains constant to justify the use of the same label 'dance' and to make the study of such disparate forms coherent?

2. Basic tools

In making proposals for a more coherent account of the possibilities of dance study it is taken for granted that there must be a relevant language structure and a notation system in order for discourse of any kind to take place. It is simply not possible to study, teach or learn about dance without a language structure which parallels (however approximately) and clarifies important concepts. Arguments concerning the relationship between language and concepts are a complex study in their own right and beyond the province of this book except in so far as they emphasis the importance of a conceptual and linguistic structure for the study of any subject.

The process of establishing an appropriate language for dance is dependent upon a method of observing and analysing typical dance movements. In turn this provides a structure of related concepts, for example, covering action possibilities, spatial location, relationships, and a qualitative or expressive range of movement.

Clearly a movement analysis of some kind is necessary but this must, for clarity, convenience of use and validity relate to the expressive purpose of the dance. ('Expressive' is used here not to mean 'self-expressive' nor as referring to an 'Expression' theory of art but in the sense that all dance is expressive— whether artistically, as ritual, socially etc.) Here the importance of the context arises again since it might be seen to be unrealistic to expect one system of analysis to fit all manifestations of dance particularly if one takes Eastern cultures into account. Perhaps in a similar way to music, where Western tonal systems are based on different structures from Eastern ones, there is a need for at least two culturally based accounts.

The fact that these questions arise and are hotly debated at the present time indicates the embryonic nature of this area of study. It is important to get at the *meaningful* nature of dance movements yet systems developed so far tend to offer detailed attention to observable features separated from 'meaning'. Perhaps there is a need for a pure movement analysis of a kind appropriate to the range of movements found in a number of dance forms (with special adaptations for other forms) and then a further level of analysis which seeks to look at the movement within the overall structure (i.e. compositional analysis) in relation to meaning or perceived significance.

There are problems here to which there is no simple, clear cut answer. On the one hand, a system based on anatomical possibilities of the human body (similar to the physics of music?) produces symbols to describe the total range of human movement, but this is unlikely to be specific enough in practice and would be cumbersome, requiring years of study to become proficient in detailed analysis. In addition it would not necessarily illuminate the dance very much in terms of meanings or compositional structure.

Other approaches start from a view of movement and/or dance as analogous with language and look for syntax systems which might help with dance analysis. The area of semiotics (the study of signs and symbols, especially the relationship between written or spoken signs and their referents in the physical world or the world of ideas) is a developing one and one used most frequently by anthropologists. A further area is that of dance semantics which is normally used to relate language and meaning by studying changes in meaning arising from different groupings of symbols.

However, the apprropriateness of all these systems is questioned by aestheticians (and people concerned with semiotics etc. are usually, though not exclusively, concerned with dance as an aesthetic/artistic phenomenon) who argue that aesthetic meaning is not a parallel with linguistic meaning, i.e. it does not arise from simply building 'meaning units' in a linguistic sense. For example, Zelinger (1979) explicitly considers this analogy of theatre dance with language. He argues, surely falsely, that linguistic-type theories can fill gaps in aesthetic theory. This must be to confuse two very different 'language games'. Perhaps there is more usefulness in the semantic approach where the dance is in a ritual/social context and a good example of this is the work of Kaeppler (1972) on Tongan dance.

Best (1978) points to the dualistic problems involved in regarding movement and meaning as two distinct entities in his book *Philosophy and Human Movement*. He is specifically criticising Metheny, but the argument seems equally valid in relation to any theory of symbolism. Best argues that just as an idea and a concept are logically tied, so movement is to meaning. Further, meaning does not arise from simple units built up, each which discrete import, but from the various sentences (contexts) in which it is used. Thus meaning 'is given by the context of the action, or complex of actions, of which it can be observed to form a part' (1978, p. 136). This is where distinctions have to be made between physical movements which may be identical in anatomical and biomechanical terms but which only have significance when viewed in context and from a particular perspective, e.g. the aesthetic or moral, and thus have different meaning.

In consequence of the development of a system of analysis, *methods of recording* movement can be developed. Although several notation systems exist the principal one used in courses in higher education is that of Kinetography or Labanotation which is closely related, of course, to the method of analysis most usually found, i.e. that based on Laban's theories.

Learning to read a script and to write notation hardly merits a place on a degree level course. In parallel with music it should merely be the taken-for-granted tool of the dance student since it is the basis of dance literacy. The lack of facility evident among students and dance tutors is the result of the traditional educational orientation and the emphasis on participation in creating something new. Similarly there is a lack of serious study of the dance itself, i.e. its choreographed structure, since there are so few scores to study. Music would be a far poorer study if there were no scores, in fact it seems almost an incredible notion, since much insight arises from analysis and interpretation of a score.

The *study* of notation systems, however, (as distinct from the act of notating) both *historically* and in relation to their *efficiency* for recording different dance forms is of course a valid theoretical exercise.

To summarise, the recording and reading of scripts is hardly a theoretical study in its own right but is a valuable and basic tool of study. Paradoxically some examining bodies are quicker to accept notation as a valid academic study than other aspects of dance, perhaps because it appears to be empirically based.

3. Central concepts

Building upon the basic tools required to talk sensibly about the area of human experience called 'dance' it is possible now to reconsider the discipline requirements outlined in Chapter I in relation specifically to dance. The existence of a collection of interests and problems which are coherently related gives the reason for an area of study, makes clear the valid concerns of that area distinct from those of any other, and explains the overlapping nature of associated concepts. 'Ideas', 'objects' and 'experiences', it was argued, might constitute interests or problems, thus in a general sense it might be theoretical notions and/or objects (man-made or natural) and/or human experiences of a particular kind which form the focus of attention.

In the study of dance it is possible to focus on any or all three of these, that is:

1. on *ideas*—notions, thoughts etc. about the place of dance in society; about the dance itself; about its human or artistic significance

2. on *objects*—which simply are the dances

3. on *experiences*—which concern the processes of making and performing dance and the impact they have on spectators.

Areas of study might concern the development of appropriate theoretical structures; the particular characteristics of the medium of movement and its manipulation into a form; or the criteria of appraisal which are relevant for a given form of dance.

These interests and issues cohere around the essentially human activity of *making, performing* and *appraising* (appreciating) the structured form of movement called dance in which there is a concern for the aesthetic appropriateness of movement beyond instrumental or extrinsic requirements. It is contended that while dance may have magical or social or other aims it is in all forms concerned with the aesthetic (ref. Ch. I).

A reminder is pertinent here of the distinctions made between 'art' and the 'aesthetic' in Chapter I in order to be clear that while all forms of dance might be said to be aesthetic they do not all fulfil the requirements of art and indeed do not exist for that purpose. It is a complication which has implications for dance in education if dance is said to be part of aesthetic education as distinct from art education. Further, the aesthetic appropriateness referred to in the previous paragraph is to do with movement—any abstract characterisation of the aesthetic requires application to concepts relevant to *dance* in general and not only to dance theatre forms.

As an example, if the aesthetic/art distinction is related to the fact of human performance as central to all forms of dance, a high level of skill within a particular theatre style is often given as a distinguishing characteristic between dance as art and other forms of dance. However, while specific technique systems, e.g. Cechetti, Graham, are relevant to certain expressive ends, varying amounts of and types of bodily skill are required in social and ritual dance, sometimes to a very high level within a narrow range of action. In other words these are not simple distinctions, the implications have yet to be fully explored.

In arguing for a broader use of relevant aesthetic terms (and against the exclusive appropriation of them by 'dance as art' theorists) one has also to include the term 'choreography'. Although most widely used in relation to theatre dance it is also used by anthropologists and others to refer to the simple fact that dances are made. There is no other term which encompasses the *making* and the made *form*.

Certainly a word is required which allows one to encompass, yet distinguish between, the dance itself, the making process and the person who makes it since different considerations come into play in studying each of these. Thus the terms a 'choreographic work', the 'choreographic process' and the 'choreographer' are relevant to all forms of dance.

In the section which follows, each of the notions of *choreography*, *performance* and *appreciation* is examined.

Choreography

A conceptual framework which emerges for the area of *choreography* must take into account both the choreographer's ability to make dances (practical knowledge) and the experience and understanding which underlies it and arises from a study of established and esteemed works. How dances are structured, what the elements of form are, and have been in different stylistic periods, is factual knowledge about which propositions can be made. The fact that they have not yet been drawn into a coherent framework which applies to dances made in different historical periods does not deny the possibility of doing so. The transience of dance, the lack of preserved dances and of experts in the field have probably contributed to the limited evidence of structure. This kind of conceptual structure in choreography is clearly necessary, just as theories of composition are needed in the study of music. While the gifted choreographer may work without apparent recourse to such knowledge the average student at school and in higher education needs to work (at least part of the time) within well tried structures, since it is through this that understanding of choreography arises.

Any 'dance making' (and any resulting dance) is covered by the term choreography. Even improvised dance exhibits 'form in the making' since in principle it is possible to repeat, fix in time and thus make 'a dance'. In some forms of dance there may be more emphasis on the moment and none or little on repetition and establishing form. In a Cage/Cunningham dialogue, for example, the improvisation shows elements of form, characteristic movement patterns extended, developed, repeated etc. If Cunningham is not making 'dance' what is he doing? One might say that he was not making *a* dance with a title which could go into a repertoire for a dance company but that would be a rather esoteric definition of dance. Whether or not an object is preserved may be more to do with economic or social structures than with dance.

The term choreography has been imbued with additional meanings peculiar to the art work, but the use of this concept in this text should be seen initially as context free.

Performance

Dance *performance* has to take account of the skills involved in bringing the dance into existence. There are two related elements in this process, one of which concerns *bodily competence* and the development of 'knowing how' to dance, and the second, *interpretation*. To the extent that *bodily competence* does not merely consist in knowing how to dance, in the sense of being able to, it exemplifies an underlying conceptual structure. There are several technique systems which would qualify although the structures are different. Classical ballet and modern dance (each with more than one variation of technique) have a technical basis which is reliant upon a set of principles. These principles vary but each system contains procedures based upon analysis of the body and, more importantly, its movement possibilities, and/or the requirements of specific dance styles formulated into training schemes. The second element of performance is concerned with *interpretation* and the skills and knowledge of the performer which contribute to a valid presentation of a particular choreographer's work. Considerable knowledge of individual style and of devices which are characteristic of a certain period are required.

Given that any dance requires a specific range of bodily skills it is possible to articulate the physical requirements for performing that dance. The level of skill required is, obviously, variable between dance genres, styles etc. as is the type of movement skill required. The physical requirements then, although they may be systematised into a structure of their own (e.g. some classical ballet systems etc.) arise out of the need for expression. This is equally relevant whether for ethnic or ritual or art dance.

Tied to the notion of skilled bodily activity for all types of dance then is that of interpretation. Since dance movement is not context-less but occurs in specific patterns, relative to the purpose of its existence in that particular context, there are contained in the notion of performance ideas about 'meaning'. In some instances there is little freedom for the performer to introduce individual variations but in others the possibility for enhancing the form is extensive. In other words the choreographic structure may be more or less specified. However, the constant aspect of interpretation is that of the performer dancing in a particular *way*, that demonstrates understanding of the stylistic conventions of a certain choreographer and/or of a period in dance history. While the same steps may appear in a social dance of the twentieth century as exist in a ballet (e.g. the waltz step) the manner of performance varies considerably.

Appreciation

Appreciation in dance would seem to involve the giving of reasons for statements made about the value and significance of particular dances. The process of coming to know a dance is through identification of salient features in relationship to the total dance. It is fundamental and obvious perhaps that this is only accomplished through repeated viewings of the dance with critical frameworks to assist the process, to point to criteria which control the construction and the effect of the various juxtaposed incidents within a dance. While, as expounded in Chapter I, there may be no single interpretation of a dance there is nevertheless a limited range of valid interpretations. Their validity can only be established by reference to the particular dance.

The act of appreciation is also used widely to encompass critical enquiry of many kinds. Clearly it is possible to orientate this towards a historical, aesthetic, social focus etc. and different theoretical frameworks would underlie it. General methods of approach, however, are common, i.e. of description, analysis, interpretation and evaluation. In dance terms it would be possible to conduct appraisal purely in a *theoretical* manner, e.g. a critical analysis of the place of dance in eighteenth century society. Further, it would be possible to conduct *practical* enquiries in this manner, e.g. the identification of the salient features of a dance, the perception of relationships between elements which give form to dance structures etc.

The purpose of critical studies is that features (observable in the dance or facts from literature) are subjected to reasoning processes in order to arrive at a clear understanding and evaluation of whatever aspect of dance is the focus of interest.

To illustrate relationships among the trio of concepts, i.e. the *making, performing* and *appreciation* of dance, the notion of appreciation or appraisal, for example, is a necessary part of both choreography and performance, but it may also be separated out as an activity in its own right. There are many forms which this appraisal may take, from the kinesthetic feedback of the dancer, to a highly developed form of critical/social/historical appreciation. But for the dance to continue to exist some form of appraisal must take place to confirm its continuing appropriateness for its purposes.

Choreography, dance performance and appreciation can be understood and characterised as nouns and as verbs, i.e. as *existent artefacts* or *objects* and as *processes* or *experiences* and, in the sense that dance is a human activity which takes place in time, the artefact and the process are insolubly bound. Trying to separate out the dancer from the performance, the choreographer from the choreography, and the critic from the appreciation is, however difficult in some cases, essential if one is to be clear about the structure, content, viable interpretations and meanings of a dance. Some would argue that since a human being performs all these acts it is impossible or irrelevant to divorce them. But it has to be *possible* otherwise rational discourse could not take place and it is *relevant* in arriving at an understanding of what is presented as dance. While personal idiosyncrasies either of style or taste (i.e. in performance or appreciation) may bring an individualistic approach they must be seen for what they are and not confused with the permanent structure of a dance. One explanation for the difficulty of this enterprise at present lies in the lack of recorded artefacts and therefore of comparable performances of a particular work.

The central organising concepts of dance are found in notions of choreography, dance performance and dance appreciation which are the major characteristic features of dance. There are further ideas subsumed under each concept which describe in more detail and relate across and between the major features. The interlocking of these sub-concepts gives a logical coherence and spells out the interrelationship of a network of concepts in a way which might be seen to satisfy the requirements of a disciplined area of study.

A reiteration of the importance of the context in which a dance form occurs is pertinent here, for the description of sub-concepts is related to, derived from and tied to dance in a particular context. One would expect to find some of the same content across several dance forms but also to find some areas omitted and new ones inserted since, for example, an art context gives a different emphasis and structure to a dance from a religious context. Further, within different dance styles subsumed under the concept of art one would expect to find some similar but some discrete concepts since expressive needs and meanings differ. In any one instance of a dance the context in which it occurs gives the appropriate perspective from which the choreography, performance and appreciation should be viewed.

Diagram 4 gives major concepts with examples of sub-concepts. All of the major concepts can be further qualified in this way by reference to sub-concepts in order to provide theoretical notions which aid study and understanding. They form an embryonic body of knowledge to be acquired. The sub-concepts relate to each of the main concepts in different ways, becoming relevant depending upon whether the focus is on choreography, performance or appreciation, and on which particular aspect of them.

For example, if one is particularly interested in the work of a choreographer, one immediately wants to know what characterises his work and distinguishes it from that of others. In pursuing this it is necessary to isolate *characteristic movements*

Diagram 4: Concepts and sub-concepts of dance study

Sub-concepts	Concepts		
	Choreography	Performance	Appreciation
	a. knowledge of/ use of particular, characteristic movements	a. ability to perform those movements technically	a. ability to perceive and order elements within a structure
	b. knowledge of appropriate expressive ends	b. understanding of range of expression likely to arise	b. evaluation of appropriateness for expressive ends
Genre	requirements and characteristics of a particular *form* of dance, e.g. tap, ballet, jazz, modern, post-modern		
Style	the *manner* in which something is expressed, the choreographic features which make e.g. a Graham dance distinct from a Hawkins or Cunningham work		
Structure	the way in which sections of a dance are put together in the interests of expressive form e.g. binary, narrative		
Devices	use of choreographic devices in order to give logic and cohesion to the form e.g. through repetition, inversion, development, resolution		

in relation to the kinds of things he makes dances about. This information has then to be placed within what is known about the *genre* in which he works, e.g. Paul Taylor has to be placed within the post Graham modern dance era, and his place within a group of artists established. The *style* of his expression is a further area of interest since it might be the manner in which movements are put together which is distinctive. In relation to form, the *structure and choreographic devices* of certain dances can be examined for pattern, repetition, inversion etc.

4. Methods of procedure and verification of success

How these concepts are learned is another matter and the left hand column of the following set of diagrams describes three major methods of becoming conversant with the dance. The concepts, sub-concepts and content remain the same, i.e. they form the conceptual framework, what differs is the approach to learning. The approach can be either by *learning about*, i.e. studying books, scores etc.; by *dancing* and experimenting with the possibilities of dance, and being taught dance studies; or by *appraising* existing and experimental work according to appropriate criteria.

Establishing that there are concepts which are centrally relevant in the study of dance and which are themselves logically related fulfils only part of the requirements laid out at the start of the book for aspiring disciplines. As soon as one is involved in the *making* of a dance, as distinct from appreciating an already existing one which can be analysed and enjoyed as a permanent artefact, one is concerned with the *process* of compositions, of the craft of putting together movements in the particular way that makes dance. Thus procedures for making dances can be demonstrated to exist and to be directly related to the nature of the thing to be made, i.e. the dance. The notion of 'performance', for example, can be studied both in a theoretical and in a practical sense of learning how to perform. Both kinds of study are relevant to an understanding of dance. These are small examples of the strands given in the diagrams but they point to one of the crucial aims of education in any disciplined activity, that of learning how to proceed in a particular area of enquiry. To be true to the nature(s) of dance one must attend to *processes* in all three areas of choreography, performance and appreciation as well as to concepts and content to be learned. This meets the second area of discipline requirements, that methods/procedures appropriate to the activity exist, can be taught and studied.

The ideas presented in Diagram 5 are based on course

Diagram 5a: Concepts in relation to methods of procedure

Methods of procedure	Examples of content derived from sub-concepts in relation to the major concept of CHOREOGRAPHY
Theoretical/ learning about	1. use of movement material, designed, given rhythm 2. dance genres e.g. classical/modern theatre, folk, ritual 3. dance styles e.g. lyric, mimetic, abstract, chance 4. dance forms e.g. free, narrative, rondo etc. 5. choreographic devices e.g. repetition, development, resolution 6. significance/meaning in art, social, ritual contexts 7. presentation e.g. use of theatrical devices in social/ritual contexts
Practical/ learning by doing	1. examples of 1-7 above from established repertoire 2. studies based on specific aspects of 1-7 3. improvisation, experimental work with 1-7 4. organisation of material to make dance pieces
Evaluative/ learning through appraisal	1. analysis of dance works in established repertoire with reference to categories 1-7 2. analysis of studies 3. appraisal of validity of experimental work 4. appraisal of constructed pieces

submissions from colleges and derived from analysis. No one institution uses a course structure which even remotely resembles this. An outline is provided rather than a definitive statement of the vast number of possibilities.

Each of these broad outlines of the study area contains a wealth of possibilities. It is only a brief summarised account which is presented here. A full working out in relation to specific dances, dancers and choreographers is the next stage of development. Whether or not it is valuable to do so depends upon taking a particular curriculum stance. If it is seen as

Diagram 5b: Concepts in relation to methods of procedure

Methods of procedure	Examples of content derived from sub-concepts in relation to the major concept of **PERFORMANCE**
Theoretical/ learning about	1. movement possibilities, range and limitations of human movement e.g. anatomical and other methods of analysis 2. principles underlying one or more systems of training 3. examples of systems which codify particular types of movement within an art, social or ritual context 4. interpretation of a given dance, criteria for valid reconstruction based on e.g. other dances of the same choreographer, same period etc.
Practical/ learning by doing	1. dance exercises based on a range of bodily activities and designed to increase mobility, strength, coordination, sensitivity, kinaesthetic feedback 2. studies structured with rhythm and dynamics in particular styles e.g. Graham, Jazz 3. performance of established repertoire and interpretation of set works
Evaluative/ learning through appraisal	1. the appropriateness of selected techniques for expressive ends 2. the nature of performance in a public sense within a theatrical/social/ritualistic context 3. the different interpretations arising from emphases in performance

desirable that a vast bank of 'content packages' is established as an aid to teaching then it is of value. Alternatively, it is reasonable to expect that the individual teacher would want the freedom to determine specific examples and content within a given, logically determined and coherent framework. It would seem essential, however, in research terms that the possibilities

Diagram 5c: Concepts in relation to methods of procedure

Methods of procedure	Examples of content derived from sub-concepts in relation to the major concept of **APPRECIATION**
Theoretical/ learning about	1. methods of critical analysis 2. underlying theories 3. relevance of particular theories to dance contexts 4. concepts peculiar to the critical context e.g. art concepts 5. general concepts common to all forms of dance appraisal
Practical/ learning by doing	1. identifying salient features 2. clarifying relationship of elements 3. writing criticism, taking account of context, through a process of description, analysis, interpretation and evaluation
Evaluative/ learning through appraisal	1. statements about the important elements of a work vis the work itself 2. statements and reasoned arguments about the relationship between elements of a work within its total framework 3. critical statements about the work in context 4. statements of value and meaning

are worked out and made available.

The third requirement of a discipline outlined in Chapter I was that there should be criteria of success arising from notions of what constitutes excellence in a sphere. In other words the public standards of the activity itself determine ultimately the standards of dance while academic standards determine the levels of aspiration of those who *study* dance. Clearly these standards have to be related to the areas of choreography, performance and appreciation.

The *methods of verification* which demonstrate that knowledge exists relate directly to the concepts and methods of procedure.

If one wishes to know what has been learned (in a conceptual sense) then this might be evaluated in discussion or through written work which reveals analytic processes as well as the ability to use concepts appropriately and to validate arguments with relevant information. Practical and theoretical knowledge might be demonstrated through performance of dance if it reveals specific skills and interpretive ability.

Both practical and theoretical kinds of knowledge are demonstrated in the making of dance, thus choreographic standards, or an understanding of choreography might be revealed in either of these ways.

The coherence of the study area in total is diagrammatically illustrated opposite.

Summary

Keeping to the notion of 'dance study' in a context-free theoretical sense, a structure is presented here of concepts, sub-concepts, methods of procedure and verification principles based around the collection of problems and interests which unifies the human activity of dance.

It is argued that this is the *only valid starting point* for an account of the study of dance. However, one immediately has to acknowledge that the dance itself, i.e. any one instance of it, exists in a particular time and place and has a function of, for example, an artistic, ritual or social nature. Therefore these perspectives and contexts are developed in the following chapter, related now to the major concepts and study methods outlined in this chapter. Specific examples of units of study illustrate the points made.

References and further reading

Adshead, J. (1980) Dance as a discipline. University of Leeds Ph.D. thesis.

Diagram 6: The coherence of the dance study area

CONCEPT	DESCRIPTION OF CONCEPT	SUB-CONCEPTS	STUDY PROCEDURES
Choreography	a. process of making dance b. product, a dance : mvt. selected, refined, given form in a style which is meaningful in relation to expressive ends : processes of selection, manipulation of material	DANCE GENRES DANCE STYLES	Theoretical study of/practical demonstration of/critical evaluation of : effective use of characteristic movements which are appropriate to certain expressive ends
Performance	a. process of performing, of executing the dance b. product, a performance : mastery of physical skills : understanding of structure, style, for interpretation	DANCE FORMS	Theoretical study of/practical demonstration of/critical evaluation of : technical requirements of performance to an effective standard in relation to : requirements of a particular expressive end
Appreciation	a. process of evaluation b. product, a piece of critical analysis : critical systems relevant to art, ritual and social accounts of dance : recognition of salient features, wholes	CHOREO-GRAPHIC DEVICES STRUCTURE	Theoretical study of/practical demonstration of/critical evaluation of : elements of structure as part of whole : in relation to requirements of expressive ends

Best, D. (1974) *Expression in movement and the arts.* London: Lepus.

Best, D. (1974) *Philosophy and human movement.* London: Allen and Unwin.

Gulbenkian Foundation (1980) *Dance education and training in Britain.*

Hanna, J.L. (1979) *To dance is human.* Austin: University of Texas.

Kaeppler, A.L. (1972) Method and theory in analysing dance structure, *Ethnomusicology,* Vol. XVI, No. 2, pp. 173-217.

Kinkeldy, O. (1929, 1966) *A Jewish dancing master of the Renaissance.* New York: Dance Horizons.

Zelinger, J. (1979) Directions for a semiotics of dance, in *Dancing and dance theory,* Ed. Preston-Dunlop, V., pp. 9-21.

CHAPTER V

Perspectives and contexts for the study of dance

1
Time and space perspectives

2
Art, ritual and social contexts

3
Diagrammatic outlines of perspectives and contexts in relation to dance study

Once it is clearly established that the dance itself, i.e. its choreography, performance and appreciation, is worth studying and that suitable methods for doing so exist then any one example of a dance has to be placed in a time and space perspective. At the beginning of the book it was maintained that the context in which any particular dance occurs determines to a significant extent the nature of the dance. Thus, while the study of the structure and choreographic devices of a dance, or of different performances is centrally important, the methods of study of meanings, criticisms, functions etc. are influenced by the place of that dance both in the perspectives of *time* and *space* and in its particular *context*.

The main purpose of this chapter is to demonstrate how perspectives and contexts both guide and control the study of dance.

1. Time and space perspectives

The *time* perspective emphasises the enduring nature of dance by taking a long term view through historical perspectives and it also *guides* the focus to relevant developments in time. Its *guiding* function is that it provides a framework that is appropriate, a particular era has a complete cultural setting and it is in the light of this that meaningful dance study takes place.

In a very simple way the *spatial* location of a dance culture is also a guiding force since geographical factors (both physical and human) give the basic conditions of life in that culture. It also provides a *controlling* mechanism since some theoretical constructs are irrelevant to one society but pertinent to another, thus it points to the appropriate direction of investigation.

There are other good reasons for a time/space perspective in the study of dance. If it is a valid aim for the study of dance that students should acquire a broad perspective as well as some depth study then it is essential that the insights of history and geography are made available. The perspectives of time and space, i.e. of the historical existence of dance across all geographical boundaries of the world, give an opportunity to approach dance in a way that is free of ethnocentricity (culture-boundness) and which allows present developments to be viewed more objectively. One could argue that the *lack* of such a perspective encourages either violent swings in what is taught in schools and colleges or a single minded emphasis on one form of dance to the exclusion of all others.

The central concepts of the dance, i.e. its choreography, performance and appreciation and the sub-concepts described previously, might be regarded as a core which is constantly moved over a three dimensional map of the world and through different periods of time and this allows a particular manifestation of dance to be examined. According to the level and requirements of particular courses (from C.S.E. to Hons. degree level) different depths of study can be catered for and different disciplines become relevant. The focus, however, remains the dance and its making, its performance(s) and appraisal in terms of its significance for that culture at that time and its value in itself.

Time and space perspectives which cut through and across all dance forms are valid studies in themselves. In addition they provide a wider cognitive framework, academically based on theoretical constructs from history and human geography*, applied to dance. A detailed study, for example, of the whole historical development of dance would of itself be an enormous undertaking but by judicious choice of examples it is possible to demonstrate the importance of a historical perspective to the understanding of the nature(s) of dance. In order to show the great width and depth of study that is possible one need only list the main cultural periods of development of Western society (bearing in mind that the equivalent depth exists for Eastern/Far Eastern cultures) and against them consider the

---

*Human geography is a shorthand term for the complex and inter-disciplinary area of study concerned.

central concepts of dance. For example:

(a) how in any one period of time was the dance made and what was it like?
(b) what features characterised its performance?
(c) who performed it and why?
(d) how was it appraised, what significance was it seen to have at the time, what was its perceived function?
(e) in general terms, how did it reflect/anticipate/subvert the development of that particular society at that time in history?
(f) how did that manifestation relate to other examples in existence concurrently?

To do this in some depth for any one society at a particular period of time could well occupy one person for two or three years of full time study—the potential resources and techniques exist. This whole area needs further elucidation in curriculum terms in relation to historical method, so that viable and relevant units of study can be created.

However, at the present time in higher education attention is given to the development of so called 'primitive man' through Greek and onto Medieval and Renaissance dance examples finishing with twentieth century forms of dance as art, notably modern dance. The inadequacies of this approach when spread over a very limited number of lectures, are obvious. Further, it is based on an evolutionary theory that Western man has developed from and become far more civilised than 'primitive man'. Hanna (1979), for example, exposes the inadequacies of this very well and points to the limitations (and arrogance) of an ethnocentric standpoint.

In a spatial sense the aim is to impart an understanding of dance as a facet within the total web of human, social existence. The purpose is to illustrate the place of dance within a society, as a system of communication and as a part of the cultural values of a society. Again it provides a means of distancing from the here and now, from the immediate concerns of dance in twentieth century Britain and allows an objective consideration of the many *different* and perfectly *valid* and *interesting* ways in which dance functions.

In addition to starting with one of the central concepts and locating the dance in time and space it is also possible, of course, to take as a *focus* of study one of the perspectives or one of the contexts of art, ritual or society. The dance is then examined from a particular standpoint and according to the structures of another discipline. This might, for example, be the history of dance where the concern is to locate changes through time to understand some specific example of dance *in the light of* previous forms, social conditions etc. Illustrations of the perspectives approach are found in Diagram 7.

2. Art, ritual and social contexts

Once a society is placed in time and space, forms of dance are further defined by the particular contexts in which they exist. The context guides attention to, for example, social, ritual or artistic areas of human endeavour. It is these *contexts*, derived from the purpose for which the dance was created, that provide the theoretical constructs which control the study process.

It has consistently been maintained throughout this text that the study of any particular example of dance has to be placed in context, and that the dance itself and any study of it is only meaningful if seen in this way. The purpose of this section is to illustrate the ways in which different contexts guide (i.e. provide the framework for) and control (i.e. govern the direction of) study of particular dance forms.

The possible contexts which give rise to dance are manifold, including social, artistic, religious, political, economic, psychological and each of these areas needs investigation, but principally (as examples of major study areas) dance exists within artistic, ritualistic and social contexts. These contexts are not unitary in their influence, that is, one context is rarely the sole construct since the same dance may exist for more than one purpose. One example of this is the court dance of the

97

seventeenth century which had both social and artistic connotations. A more complicated case is that of, for example, religious dance (akin to religious paintings or music created for church services) where artistic requirements may be finely balanced with the expression of appropriate religious sentiments. Further, such works have usually been commissioned thus providing a livelihood for the artist/craftsman but also influencing what was made.

Similarly, art forms of dance are used in a ritual context, within worship and/or in religious settings. Currently performers are invited by churches to perform dances based on suitable themes. The performers may have no religious convictions but in their roles as artists portray and interpret faith, belief, prayer, in a way designed to encourage religious fervour in the spectators, thus it is not solely an art experience but has religious overtones. Unless this was the case it would hardly be performed in a church and with the blessing of church officials anyway.

There are further complexities arising from these areas of contextual study. For example, if the main concern is with a particular period in the history of dance it is still necessary to locate the dance in a particular context. Thus while a *perspective* may start the enquiry a *context* is immediately necessary since this gives the function of any specific dance form. For example, it is possible to look at the history of dance as *art*, or as part of man's culture, or as *ritual*. Further, if one started with an interest in dance within a ritual context it would also be necessary to be aware of historical changes in ritual and also of the attitudes of different cultures to both dance and ritual. One then identifies an area for deeper study if the dance itself is to be examined. A diagrammatic outline of each of the contexts is given in Diagram 8. The purpose is to show areas of study which might be profitable for dance, to illustrate the theoretical requirements of a particular context in relation to the dance itself and to point to relevant study procedures derived from Chapter IV.

The first context on the diagram is that of *art*. Since this has received greater consideration than any other context throughout the book it is unnecessary to expand further. A brief description of the current positions of the ritual and social contexts follows before the diagram.

The *ritual context* of dance belongs chiefly to the past in Western societies although not of course in other cultures. There has, however, been a revival of interest in recent years in the Western world in the use of dance within church services and in performances of dance based on religious themes. 'Ritual' offers a broader approach which subsumes particular examples of religious systems and includes a sociological element and a personal/therapeutic one. Such an approach encompasses the study of folk forms of dance which have ritual meaning, e.g. English Sword and Hobby dances.

The important concepts and theoretical structures which inform this area of study are derived from theology and related religious studies. An anthropological standpoint is particularly important in this area since the diversity of ritual dance is greater elsewhere than in Britain.

The area of study which concerns the *social* context is vast, and at the present time, poorly developed theoretically. As a suggested model for 'Dance in society' it seems that three strands might be identified, i.e. those which concern:

(a) the individual and his relationship with society in terms of such notions as interaction and communication in relation to dance,

(b) the structures of a society in terms of institutions, organisations, groupings, and the function of dance within them,

(c) the value systems and mores underlying the workings of a social system, and the role dance plays in the transmission of them.

Anthropologists and sociologists provide the theoretical constructs in this area. As with other contexts, it is difficult enough for dance theorists to be knowledgeable about dance

Diagram 7: Historical and geographical perspectives and the study of dance

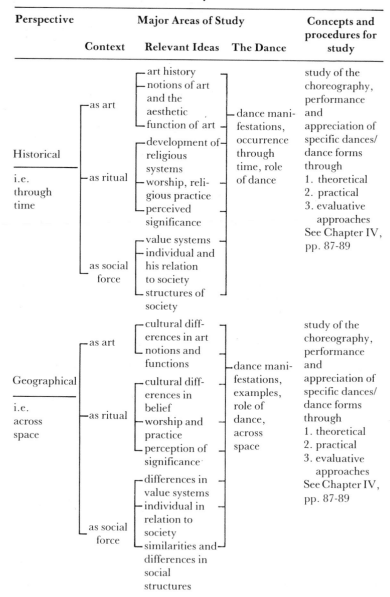

Perspective	Major Areas of Study			Concepts and procedures for study
	Context	Relevant Ideas	The Dance	
Historical —————— i.e. through time	as art	art history notions of art and the aesthetic function of art	dance manifestations, occurrence through time, role of dance	study of the choreography, performance and appreciation of specific dances/dance forms through 1. theoretical 2. practical 3. evaluative approaches See Chapter IV, pp. 87-89
	as ritual	development of religious systems worship, religious practice perceived significance		
	as social force	value systems individual and his relation to society structures of society		
Geographical —————— i.e. across space	as art	cultural differences in art notions and functions	dance manifestations, examples, role of dance, across space	study of the choreography, performance and appreciation of specific dances/dance forms through 1. theoretical 2. practical 3. evaluative approaches See Chapter IV, pp. 87-89
	as ritual	cultural differences in belief worship and practice perception of significance		
	as social force	differences in value systems individual in relation to society similarities and differences in social structures		

Diagram 8: Art, ritual and social contexts and the study of dance

Context	Major Areas of Study		Concepts and procedures for study
	Relevant Disciplines— Examples	The Dance	
Art	┌the — aesthetic ├ art └the arts┘	relevant aspects of philosophy (aesthetics), aesthetic concepts, criteria for work of art, theories of criticism, classificatory similarities and differences etc.	manifestations of dance as aesthetic (social etc.) as art (theatre forms), relation of dance with other arts	
Ritual	┌ritual practice ├ religious systems └significance of ritual	relevant aspects of theology, anthropology, sociology, psychology and physiology dealing with religious experience, belief systems, the supernatural etc.	manifestations of dance as ritual, in worship and in folk customs	study of the choreography, performance and appreciation of specific dances/dance forms through 1. theoretical 2. practical 3. evaluative approaches See Chapter IV, pp. 87-89
Social	┌individual in relation to society ├ value systems └structures of society	relevant aspects of philosophical anthropology, anthropology, social psychology, sociology dealing with culture, context etc.	manifestations of dance as a social force, transmitting culture, consolidating and differentiating, in interpersonal communication (social dance forms)	

Diagram 9: Examples of dance topics developed

Dance Topic	PERSPECTIVES		CONTEXTS
	Historical/ Time	Geographical/ Space	Major/Minor

WALTZ

Choreography: turning, var. in speed : step : style : close couple e.g.: Viennese, Boston, Hesitation *Performance:* technical requirements, skills Expressive style *Appreciation:* criteria for a 'good' waltz Place and significance in social and artistic contexts	*Origins:* Bavarian Landler/French Volta, evidence for and against *Development:* as court/social form : as artistic form e.g. Petipa 'Raymonda' Isadora Duncan 'Blue Danube' Dalcroze 'Invit. to the Waltz'	*Location:* West. European C18 Comparisons, German, French and English forms As reflection of particular society	*Sociology:* social life of C19, 1812 Almack's and other assembly rooms to Hunt/ State/Society/popular examples of early C20 Attitudes towards dance and relationships between sexes Rel. to religious attitudes *Aesthetics:* classical/ romantic ballet function for group episodes, concepts of beauty, lyricism harmony etc. C20 pas de deux use e.g.: Fokine 'Les Sylphides' Music influence and relationship e.g.: Strauss, Chopin

DORIS HUMPHREY 1895-1958

Choreography: 110 (approx.) works, theories of composition e.g.: 1928 Water Study, 1931 Shakers, 1936 With my red fires Characteristic mvts., structure, expressive style *Performance:* underlying principles of movement, technical requirements Stylistic features, inter- pretive requirements e.g.: study of film versions *Appreciation:* contemporary criticism e.g.: Martin, Moore Recent criticism of reconstructions e.g.: Dance Magazine March, 1979	*Origins:* early C20 modern dance, Denishawn *Development:* as contemporary of Graham : prevalent ideas about movement e.g. psychological theories of Delsarte	*Location:* United States of America Comparison with European modern dance e.g.: Laban, Wigman Similarities and differences As reflection of a particular society	*Artistic:* prevalent notions of art and the aesthetic; relevance of D.H.'s work to theories of dance as expression, social comment; stress on movement, relation with other arts, particularly music; theories of relations *Social:* art movements of the 1920s and 1930s; prevailing attitudes to dance

within the proposed theoretical framework

EDUCATIONAL RELEVANCE/ STUDY PROCEDURES	SELECTED REFERENCES
Allows study of original documents: polemic and teaching manual Allows reconstruction of a variety of manifestations, study of choreog. structure Allows performance, practical involvement in acquiring skills appropriate to particular form Allows interpretation, through different expressive natures of types Allows literature review, historical, sociological, aesthetic appraisal and evaluation e.g. : study in depth of one modern example through notation, video, live performance, prac. reconstruction, theoretical evaluation	Gen. History: Kirstein L. A short history of classic theatrical dancing. 1935, 1974 Social history: Richardson P.J.S. The social dances of the 19th century. 1960 Rust F. Dance in society. 1969 Quirey B. May I have the pleasure. 1976 Criticism: Brahms, C. Footnotes to the ballet. 1936 Coton, A.V. Writings on dance, 1938-68. 1975 Haskell, A.L. Balletomania. 1934 MacDonald, N. Diaghilev observed. 1975
Allows study of original choreography through film, notated scores, criticism and general dance writings Allows practical reconstruction of D.H.'s choreography; performance and interpretation Allows practical work in the style of D.H. using her theories of composition Allows evaluation of a theory of composition expounded in original writings Allows evaluation of D.H.'s choreography in the context of art and in social and historical contexts e.g. : study in depth of one dance for which all resources are available; Shakers etc.	Biography: Cohen, S.J. An artist first. 1972 King, E. Transformations. 1978 Theories: Humphrey, D. The art of making dances. 1959 Cohen, S.J. Dance as a theatre art. 1974 Works: Complete scores. Dance Notation Bureau Technique: Stodelle, E. The dance technique of Doris Humphrey. 1978 Criticism: Dance Magazine, March 1979 Jowitt, D. Dance beat, 1976 Siegel, M. The shapes of change, 1979

itself, let alone become aestheticians or sociologists. What is needed is the application of scholarly insights from these disciplines in the way in which, for example, Royce and Hanna have worked. It is not appropriate that every dance teacher becomes an anthropologist any more than that he or she becomes an aesthetician.

3. Diagrammatic outlines of perspectives and contexts in relation to dance study

Diagram 7 shows the historical and geographical perspectives taken as starting points. The emphasis is respectively on change through time and on similarities and differences between different cultures. The perspectives are taken through the three contexts of art, ritual and society, relevant ideas are given in note form, and the dance orientation explained. The column 'concepts and study procedures' points to the possibilities of study and methods of procedure when the central concepts of choreography, performance and appreciation are the focus of attention (ref. Chapter IV, pp. 87-89). Diagram 8 follows the same pattern but from the starting point of the contexts.

To draw together the ideas of Chapter IV, i.e. of central concepts, with those of this Chapter, i.e. of perspectives and contexts, diagram 9 starts from the dance itself and uses the appropriate perspectives and contexts to illuminate the dance. The first one takes a specific type of dance—the waltz. Clearly one could take a choreographer, as the second example does, or a dance style, a recognised dance step etc. etc., as points of interest, and much might be gained from planning units of study in this way since it is always the dance which controls the investigation rather than some other discipline. Other disciplines then become relevant at the appropriate point. The availability of scores featured in the Humphrey example is an exciting development which makes possible the study of structure in choreography in a depth which is not feasible through video alone.

Any of these proposed units of study could be pursued at many levels, for example, the C.S.E. pupil could (with suitable resources) make a meaningful attempt at many of the smaller areas within the total. At the other extreme any one small part could be the basis of an M.Phil. or Ph.D. thesis. The difference lies in the depth of study and the extent to which relationships can be made with other dances/art movements/social developments etc.

Some study possibilities are outlined here, the minute detail is fascinating and would require years of sound dance scholarship to fill in the details and develop such courses. But, in the meantime, what, in curriculum development terms, can one conclude about the study of dance? Chapter VI raises some of the main areas to be considered and points to possible directions of progress.

References

Hanna, J.L. (1979) *To dance is human.* Austin: University of Texas.

Royce, A.P. (1977) *The anthropology of dance.* London: Indiana.

CHAPTER VI

Implications for dance education

The proposed framework

The argument presented here is that it is possible (and desirable) that dance itself, and not only related disciplines, should be studied. It might seem strange to have to say this, particularly to primary or secondary school teachers or those in the private sector since, in some senses, this is what they have been doing. But there is a much fuller sense in which the dance itself can be studied, as demonstrated in the earlier part of this text. In *higher education* (state sector) examinations, viability and validity pressures have encouraged heavy reliance on other structures, usually derived from aesthetics and to a lesser extent sociology. Although lip service has been paid for a few years now to the notions of choreography, performance and appreciation there has been little follow through of the implications of these concepts in curriculum terms, hence the confusions and arguments which abound.

To explain again, the choice of a dance form or topic for study determines the parameters of that study because the appropriate frameworks are given by the initial choice. That is, the form of dance itself has structures, it has requirements embedded in the choreography and performance which can be learned. These are the criteria and the concerns which make that form of dance, or the actual dance itself, distinctive from any other. In a narrow sense of 'appreciation', the techniques and concepts are also provided by the dance itself, i.e. those which determine whether it is a good example of its type. The function which the dance performs gives the appropriate kind of appraisal of a broader kind, e.g. if it functions as art, then an artistic context is the background and in turn this provides criteria for its appreciation in a wide sense.

The perspectives and contexts illustrate the importance of the circumstances in which the dance arises. They are, of themselves, valid forms of study without which an *understanding* of the nature and function of a particular form of dance is unlikely. The proposed theoretical structure, based on concepts of choreography, performance and appreciation also gives an account of the methods of procedure which are relevant for studying different topics. Procedures of a theoretical, practical and evaluative nature can be applied and the appropriateness of the method is determined by the topic and what it is that one wishes to understand.

However, the main platform of argument is that the most serious lack in dance education is the study of the dance, i.e. its choreography, performance and appreciation. A smattering of technique(s) and a practical attempt at composition is hardly adequate to count as dance education. Nor is it likely to lead to appreciation of dance in any broad sense.

One of the major problems which bedevils such attempts to study the dance itself is the emphasis on *training dancers* rather than on *studying dance*. The influence of the major private sector dance colleges and modern dance companies is partly the cause combined with the American example. There should, of course, be suitable training for dancers and the opportunity for them to retrain later in other areas of dance education, but to focus only on training for performance distorts the nature of study, of careful, academic approaches to learning. There is certainly *a* place for performing skills within some dance courses but this place is determined by the aims and nature of that course. It seems most inappropriate that degrees (B.A., B.Ed. etc.) should be awarded *solely* on evidence of the ability to perform to a high standard in one style of dance. In general, educational aims are concerned with the development of *understanding*, whatever the level of the education system. Thus even a course which explicitly focuses on 'performance', as many combined subject courses do, has to concern itself with theoretical structures. These structures are both conceptual in considering what constitutes performance and what its distinguishing characteristics are, and technical, i.e. to do with different training structures. Both the concepts of performance and the training system are meaningless except in the context of an expressive style so immediately the choreographed work assumes importance and the concern is no longer solely with performance. It is also important that the notion of performance is extended to take in interpretation skills. This implies considerable theoretical knowledge of genre, style, a choreographer's repertoire, the ability to reconstruct from notation and to select appropriate ways of performing particular works by analysis of possible interpretations. The lack of such study can be attributed (charitably) to a lack of resources, but it is also due to a form of arrogance which arises from the view that what is produced here and now by students has some artistic value over and above established works even when students rarely see dances performed by others. This demonstrates the impoverished concepts currently operating in both higher and secondary education.

At the other end of the spectrum and in contrast with the example of a course which emphasises performance it is possible and reasonable to conceive of a course in dance which involved the student in no practical dancing and which consisted of a theoretical study of dance, for example, as a social force within a historical perspective. Concern with choreography, performance and appreciation would be from a theoretical stance with a view to understanding the occurrence of different forms of dance prevalent at various periods in history. The forms of dance studied would be determined by the society and period under investigation. The relevant theoretical constructs would be drawn from sociology, social-psychology, anthropology, history and religious studies.

The suggestion here is that a wealth of possibilities has yet to be explored. It would seem that there is a place in education for a variety of types of courses in dance which emphasise different areas of the subject, i.e. choreography, performance and appreciation, and which study them with varying combinations of theoretical, practical and evaluative approaches.

In terms of *what* is to be taught, it is possible to study any of these areas, the choreography, performance, and appreciation of a particular form, each by itself, or placed within a space/time perspective and to consider the context(s) of the dance. Different forms of dance or topics of interest will offer more and less of substance in each of these areas. It is necessary to have a broad enough map of the possible area of study in order to make valid selections in relation to any curriculum. In the face of the wealth of possibilities of study demonstrated through the structures presented here, the inadequacies of the present higher education system are evident. Teachers just do not exist who could begin to initiate pupils into this width and depth of study. Perhaps it is unrealistic to expect secondary school teachers to have this kind of background as a result of the present structure of initial training. What is essential is that teachers can return for inservice training to acquire different expertise or to deepen understanding. A logical consequence of such a recommendation is that there would have to be people able to teach these teachers and the present college system seems unlikely to provide them except in a few isolated instances. A vast expansion of *types* (not necessarily numbers) of Hons. B.Ed. and B.A. and Masters degrees would seem to be essential.

Justifications for teaching dance

It has been demonstrated that it is now mainly as an *art form* that dance is justified in the state education system and, in parallel with other art forms, it adopts an artistic/aesthetic rationale. However, if *dance itself* is worth studying, then cognisance has to be taken of the fact that only *one* of its contexts is art. To study dance only in this way is to leave uncovered much of the potential of dance study.

The term 'aesthetic education' is sometimes used in order to encompass all forms of dance, and indeed many other activities, and the consequences of this approach have yet to be explored fully. There are doubts as to the possibility of 'aesthetic education' in any meaningful sense since it can amount to no more than taking a particular attitude to any object or experience whatsoever. More narrowly one would build in conditions, i.e. that taking such an attitude is more or less relevant to the thing one is looking at, that the object or event is likely to repay that kind of attention, as distinct from (or as well as) taking a moral or political stance to it.

It is accepted that 'aesthetic education' is a broader notion than art education in applying to all forms of dance but in a different sense 'art education' is wider than aesthetic education in that it embraces the historical and social development of particular forms and their relations with each other.

The insistence on the part of dance educators that dance as art is the focus avoids issues to do with the eclectic nature of dance and it is possible therefore that the art yoke might turn out to be as constricting as the P.E. one once was.

This would seem to be the case where the context of art is acknowledged but its breadth and richness is ignored or limited in application through lack of time, suitably qualified staff and appropriate resources. For example, a degree course in any other performing art which focused entirely on its manifestation in only the last thirty years would be seen to be restricting and lacking in a necessary broad cultural perspective, yet many dance courses are of this kind.

It seems to be just as narrow minded to insist that the *only* form of dance worth teaching is dance as art, usually restricted further to a sub-species of American modern dance, as arguments for the position from which this has grown, i.e. that dance is movement and, therefore, it is part of physical education. It could be argued that not only is the art orientation a minute part of the relevance of dance to society but also that it is of far less human significance than, for example, a socio-historical study.

The teaching situation

It is perhaps the function of another book to pursue the implications of the structures presented in Chapters IV and V into specific teaching situations. When basic principles and structures have been laid out informed curriculum decisions can take place and these decisions depend upon the individual circumstances of the educational situation. There is no attempt here to lay down a definitive dance curriculum, the examples in the text are merely illustrations of how the theoretical structures might be used in practice in a way which would allow serious study. 'Serious study' is not necessarily solely theoretical. It is argued that practical and evaluative modes of learning are also important.

Furthermore, many of the contentious issues, e.g. of the teaching of technique, and of the relationship between theoretical and practical studies, which have come to dominate discussions in dance education, are resolved by taking a wider view of dance itself supported by a coherent account of the structures underlying dance study. Even within the limitations of an art context it is readily apparent that a bodily training on its own is totally inadequate as 'dance education' but conversely, that it nonetheless has a place, since skill of a certain, very specific kind is necessary in order to participate in the activity. However, this assumes that participation is desirable, and it may not always be. The validity of practical involvement would have to be argued in relation to the aims of the course. It is also necessary to bear in mind that a certain level of skill is required for *all* forms of dance, not just art forms. In other words technical proficiency/bodily competence has to be seen within a curriculum framework which puts forward a particular kind of dance education.

If the area of dance study is well defined and the emphasis is on *study* rather than involvement with dance, for example, as a therapeutic experience or as part of the socialisation process, then it is possible (indeed essential) to view the dance itself in a more detached way, to stand back and consider its objective features. Of course one wants students to enjoy their courses and to become committed to dance but this must be on the basis of knowledge and understanding as well as emotional or aesthetic response.

Training the teachers

In schools, and in college courses where teachers are trained, there are considerations other than the purely structural which influence the selection of curriculum content. These chiefly concern the type of justification offered for the study of dance within the school system. It was argued in Chapter II that general educational ideas influence the direction that dance studies take in the state education sector and although C.S.E. dance and now 'O' level syllabuses exist, the most usual curriculum pattern is still a practical, creative dance unit. There are historical reasons for the emphasis on a particular kind of dance taught in a guided discovery/creative setting. In consequence, a form of dance which claimed a uniquely educational nature came to be dominant, i.e. modern educational dance. In a strange way 'education' became elevated to a context in its own right similar to the art, ritual and social ones. This is hardly tenable since subjects taught in schools reflect, and relate to, the 'real' world, education in this sense is parasitic upon the major forms of human activity and enquiry. Thus dance in education must draw upon forms of the dance in the 'real' world for its areas of study. Theoretically, any form of dance *could* be taught. In practice, prevailing educational philosophies in combination with the interests and capabilities of staff determine what *is* taught.

In contrast the private sector dance teacher has been totally concerned with the kind of dance training appropriate to the professional, 'dance as art', world and has placed the emphasis on the acquisition of a high level of bodily competence. Until very recently this was further limited to the classical ballet field. The arguments which follow apply equally to the private and public sectors where they claim to offer a *dance education* as distinct from a training in one style of dance.

Clearly teachers may have relatively little opportunity to work in depth, but what is crucial is that in their initial training they are given some breadth of vision of what is possible, of the potential of study. Not only is it important to develop knowledgeable, appreciative dance audiences (for the dance of Eastern and other cultures as well as that of Western Europe) but also to supply notators, critics, dance aestheticians, dance historians, anthropologists etc. While careers in these areas are likely to be few it is the case that demand is increasing.

There is another, quite different, line of argument which can be made. This is, that education ought to provide a means of developing analytical qualities of mind in pursuit of an interest rather than a narrow vocational training that will be out of date in a short time. If this can be argued satisfactorily (and it is the basis of all non-vocational university education) then it is as valid to study dance history as any other kind of history. No-one would claim, or even think it desirable, that all graduates with degrees in music, English or history should only take up posts directly related to the subject of study.

The need for research

The first question raised in this text was, is there anything to study anyway? Demonstrably there is plenty of *dance* to study although the present level of scholarship about it is not high. There is a pressing need for basic research into the areas of choreography, performance and appreciation in order to work out the structures and relationships between these concepts in sufficient detail to provide a 'bank' of potential study material, drawing on examples from many forms of dance. Publication of good texts is also urgently needed, in association with relevant video and notation material. The work of experts, in aesthetics, anthropology, sociology and other functional contexts in which dance exists, needs to be related specifically to dance so that the insights which these disciplines can provide might be used in a realistic way at different levels of the study process. Again this is a matter for research.

APPENDIX A

Institutions of higher education included in the study

Former name	New name (where relevant)
Alsager College of Education	Crewe and Alsager College
Anstey College of P.E.	City of Birmingham Polytechnic Anstey Dept. of P.E.
Avery Hill College of Ed.	Avery Hill College
Bedford College of P.E.	Bedford College of Higher Ed.
Bingley College of Ed.	Ilkley College
Birmingham Univ. Dept. of P.E.	
Bishop Lonsdale Coll. of Ed.	Derby-Lonsdale College of Higher Ed.
Cardiff College of Ed.	South Glamorgan Institute of Higher Ed.
Chelsea College of P.E.	Brighton Polytechnic
City of Leeds & Carnegie Coll of Ed.	Leeds Polytechnic Carnegie School
Coventry College of Ed.	Warwick University
Crewe College of Ed.	Crewe and Alsager College
Dartford College of Ed.	Thames Polytechnic, Dartford Coll. of Ed.
Dartington College of Arts	
Digby Stuart Coll. of Ed.	Roehampton Institute of Higher Education (R.I.H.E.)
Dunfermline Coll. of P.E.	
Froebel Institute of Ed.	R.I.H.E.
Glamorgan Coll of Ed.	Polytechnic of Wales
Goldsmiths' College, University of London	

Former name	New name (where relevant)
Hull Univ. Dept. of Drama	
I.M. Marsh College of P.E.	Liverpool Polytechnic
Jordanhill College of Ed., Scottish School of P.E.	
Laban Art of Movement Centre	Laban Centre for Movement & Dance
Lady Mabel College of Education	Sheffield Polytechnic
Leeds Univ. Dept. of P.E.	
Leicester Coll. of Ed.	Leicester Polytechnic
London College of Dance and Drama	
Manchester Univ. Dept. of P.E.	
Matlock College of Ed.	
Nonington Coll. of P.E.	
Ripon Coll. of Ed.	College of Ripon & York St. John
Rolle College	
St. John's, York	College of Ripon & York St. John
St. Mark & St. John	Plymouth Polytechnic. College of St. Mark & St. John
St. Mary's College, Cheltenham	(North) Gloucestershire Institute of Higher Ed.
Southlands Coll. of Ed.	R.I.H.E.
Trent Park Coll. of Ed.	Middlesex Polytechnic—Faculty of Ed. & Performing Arts
Trinity & All Saints Colleges	
Whitelands Coll. of Ed.	R.I.H.E.
Worcester Coll. of Ed.	Worcester Coll. of Higher Ed.

APPENDIX B

Dance tutors' perceptions of C.N.A.A. validation

The growing influence of C.N.A.A. as a validating body emerged during the course of the research, and it was seen as an important area to investigate further. Consequently a questionnaire relating to validation was sent to those colleges changing to C.N.A.A. validation, in order to elicit in more detail the effect of C.N.A.A. validation on the curriculum in dance. Dance tutors were invited to describe validation procedures with no implied criticism either of the C.N.A.A. or of previous university validation. Subsequently this information was used to clarify the extent and direction of the influence of validation processes on courses in dance.

It was clear from the responses obtained that colleges submitting courses in dance found ready acceptance of the subject as a suitable area of study in higher education 'as long as the submission is clear in terms of objectives, syllabus, feasibility and staffing' (quote is from a college dance tutor).

College staff teaching dance were asked if they felt that the panels had a coherent policy about the content of dance courses. Replies indicated that on the whole there was no particular policy or view put forward and that individual members of the panels differed in the stress they placed on different aspects of dance. Some felt that this was a strength of the C.N.A.A., while others considered that it caused frustration and confusion.

Further questions concerned the differences perceived by college dance tutors between previous university validation and that of the C.N.A.A. Two respondents stated unequivocally that their universities would not accept the kind of dance courses they wished to offer or that the university would not validate non-teaching courses, hence the move to the C.N.A.A. The majority stated that the Council was more flexible in its approach but very much more stringent in its requirements. Staff teaching dance were aware that starting afresh with a new validating body would, of necessity, require more detailed planning and justification than continuing in relation to a university where personnel and courses were already known. However, unease was expressed about the minute detail required by the C.N.A.A. in as far as it implied a lack of confidence in the lecturers' ability (whereas the university had 'trusted' college staff), and requirements were seen to be contradictory in some cases. Nonetheless college dance tutors felt that the content of their courses had been affected only to a limited extent and that they had been able to do what they had wished to do.

Dance tutors were asked whether they felt that the C.N.A.A. panels had actively encouraged or opposed or were neutral to certain issues and kinds of structure for courses. The results are tabulated opposite and overleaf.

Since six of the college and university staff of the institutions involved in this study were also validators for college courses in their capacity as university staff and/or as members of C.N.A.A. panels, it was possible to ascertain the validators' view of the process. It was seen as important by validators that courses could be justified by staff in terms of aims and objectives. Validators expected dance tutors to identify their own criteria and base courses on these. One validator felt that the C.N.A.A. dance panel's wide experience, which reflected its members' deep involvement with different forms of dance, was a strength, but that college dance tutors were consequently subjected to a 'battery of views which could be confusing'. Another validator commented that:

> . . . *individual validators can and do exert a strong influence.*

continued on page 124

Table 6: Attitudes of C.N.A.A. panels to courses in dance (as perceived by dance tutors) in sampled institutions

(i) Emphasis within course	No. of tutors		
	encouraged	opposed	neutral
a) curriculum structures allowing greater student choice	5	1	1
b) an integrated/interdisciplinary approach	6	1	1
c) student involvement in practical creative processes	7		1
d) theoretical studies in dance	5		2
e) specific techniques or styles of dance	4		2
f) distinctions between the study of dance and its application to teaching	4		2

(ii) Dance content	encouraged	opposed	neutral
a) philosophy and aesthetics in relation to dance and other arts	6		2
b) psychology and psychological aesthetics in relation to dance	4		3
c) psycho-social areas relevant to dance	3		3
d) sociological and anthropological studies of dance	5		2
e) general studies of 'performing arts'	3	1	3
f) dance technique, styles and process of composition	7		1
g) history of dance and dances from particular periods	5		2
h) dance in education	4		3
i) other: notation	2		
: accompaniment	1		

The experience of submitting courses to the C.N.A.A. was described by respondents in the following way:

The Challenge	The Constraints
'valuable experience of reappraisal with opportunity for change'.	'very slow process, many frustrations, courses appear to be validated at the whim of the panel, whose members are rarely all present'.
'the total exercise has been refreshing and rewarding'.	'advice over emphasised the logistics of the situation' e.g. 2 courses per tutor maximum 'need to stress the theoretical clouded what might otherwise have been a sensible if radical approach to planning new courses'.
'demanding in time and concentration, professionally stimulating and the outcome satisfying. An opportunity to construct a course which catered for unique regional factors'. (Scotland)	
'gains in staff battling their way through to expressing what they really intended in detail'.	'frustrating because of lack of awareness of detail required'.
'has brought a new way of looking at dance—as an art form in education'.	
'a really stimulating challenge and most helpful for clarifying ideas which were previously by intuition'.	

The Challenge	The Constraints

'a most challenging and
rewarding experience, making
each one of the subject group
very aware of dance as a field
of study at first degree level
and beyond'.

'exhausting and demanding,
examining aims and content,
rigorous academic exercise'.

'insistence on high staff
qualifications in all areas'.

'procedure, conditioned by
careful scrutiny and requiring
detailed planning . . .
is clearly desirable and healthy
in the present climate'.

'the demand for aims, justifications and lucidity have made
us examine ourselves with a
rigour that is quite new and is
undoubtedly good in itself, it
has forced everyone, particularly
the inexperienced, to adopt
analytical procedures that
become a growing point'.

'of time—affects fundamental
philosophy of movement studies,
concerned for the future of
movement as experience and
knowledge in its own right'.

'a challenge'.

'it brought the staff concerned
together in discussion of the
fundamental principles and aims
and in clarifying objectives it
produced a considerable
discussion in terms of assessment
work'.

'easier to do what we wanted
to do'.

Where this is shown in terms of preference for one or other dance style rather than the ability of the staff to teach the syllabus this is potentially dangerous. Two validators of different persuasions can modify each others views and indeed the working together is making for greater understanding and sympathy between diverse views.

The view was put forward that in trying to widen dance courses, lack of sound knowledge had led to theoretical aspects being included which in some cases were irrelevant and inadequately related to dance practice. While a broad course, which at least put dance in a perspective and gave particular studies a context, was valuable one validator felt that it was essential that each college should identify core experiences which are fundamental to dance in order to give students a 'basic literacy' from which a series of option courses could develop interests in a more specific way. This literacy might include 'basic theoretical aspects; practical experience of a few styles of dance in order to appreciate the eclectic nature of dance; some bodily training or technique; and experiences in creating dances and performing others' choreography'.

In the Combined Studies area the boards of the C.N.A.A. tend to approve courses which allow for study in depth of one art with supporting studies in other arts areas. It was felt that the need to respect the integrity of each art had to be seen against the aim of fostering respect and understanding between the arts. Wherever integration was proposed it was seen as important by the board that it should be based on competence in the separate disciplines involved. The nub of the problem was seen to be to determine where the focus of the course lay; for example, whether on performance or understanding or integration. Understanding could be seen to have a historical, social or critical focus. Debate continues about whether a degree is an appropriate award for courses with professional (performing) objectives. The boards' experience suggests that staff formulating courses in this area are unclear about their objectives.

Index